STILL WITH YOU

VIOLETTA ARMOUR

STILL WITH YOU

iUniverse books may be ordered through booksellers or by contacting:

iUniverse
1663 Liberty Drive
Bloomington, IN 47403
www.iuniverse.com
1-800-Authors (1-800-288-4677)

Because of the dynamic nature of the Internet, any web addresses or links contained in this book may have changed since publication and may no longer be valid. The views expressed in this work are solely those of the author and do not necessarily reflect the views of the publisher, and the publisher hereby disclaims any responsibility for them.

Any people depicted in stock imagery provided by Getty Images are models, and such images are being used for illustrative purposes only. Certain stock imagery © Getty Images.

ISBN: 978-1-5320-7697-8 (sc)
ISBN: 978-1-5320-7698-5 (e)

Print information available on the last page.

iUniverse rev. date: 06/10/2019

To Kathleen,

Dedication

"Trust in the Lord with all your heart & lean not on your own understanding"

To the loyal readers of my first book, *I'll Always Be With You*. Your kind words and encouragement inspired me to write this sequel. I hope it does not disappoint in any way.

While writing the sequel, I lost two loves and I dedicate this book to them.

To my husband Don, who supported all my endeavors throughout our thirty-two year marriage.
To Jim Johnson, who was the first to open my heart after Don.

I was twice blessed.

Violetta Armour

Introduction
September 2001 New York City

The pulse of Times Square beats loudly for Luther. Louder than the skyscrapers and landmarks of Chicago he is more familiar with—the Sears Tower, the John Hancock Building, Water Tower and the Magnificent Mile along Lake Shore Drive. And the New York city beat is intensified because he is sharing it with his bride of one-year, Marletta.

Luther and Marletta delayed their honeymoon until she finished her Master's degree. When they discovered a Peace Corps information meeting in New York City they planned their travel dates so they could attend that also. The idea of traveling to foreign countries appeals to them before they start a family.

They arrive in the city Saturday night, September 8, and check into their beautiful suite at the Marriott in Times Square. They walk the Square at midnight with all the glittering lights lit up like Las Vegas. It's a far cry from Main Street in Middleburg, Indiana, where they live.

Sunday, September 9, they sleep in and order room service for breakfast so they can enjoy their luxurious suite for a few hours, counting the yellow taxis that look like Match Box cars from their twelfth-story window. All lined up bumper to bumper, they inch along. Although the blaring horns are muted through the glass window, Luther imagines the continuous honking if they were street side.

Luther and Marletta spend the rest of the day at MOMA, the Museum of Modern Art, they had heard so much about. They enjoy a romantic dinner Sunday night in Little Italy where a violin player serenades them with "Bella Notte" when he learns of their honeymoon.

"I feel like we should be eating the same string of spaghetti like *Lady and the Tramp,* Luther says to Marletta.

"I'm game." She stretches a long piece of pasta between her fingers and offers the other end to Luther. Their lips meet in the middle for a brief kiss. Brief because they are laughing. Life is good.

Monday, September 10, they take a horse-drawn carriage ride through Central Park and have lunch at Tavern on the Green. Then they search out the deli where Seinfeld's Soup Nazi roars at the people in line, "No soup for you!"

Monday afternoon is the trip to Ellis Island where Luther traces his ancestors' journey from Bulgaria. In the computer room, he finds the manifest that lists his great grandfather's name, Variky Kostoff, 1921, on the ocean liner, *The Baltic.*

During his courtship with Marletta, Luther shared the story of his parents' high-school interracial and forbidden romance in the sixties that resulted in his birth. Variky was the grandfather of Stan, the white boy his black mother loved but never married. Luther was only recently told that Stan was his father when his widow, Mary, and three children moved back to their hometown of Middleburg. Suddenly Luther had a whole new family—Teddy, his seventeen-year-old half-brother and two little sisters, Ruby, age eight and Cathy, age five. The half siblings were new to him, but they were yet to be told of his relationship to them. Teddy only knows Luther as his high-school basketball coach.

Luther and Marletta decide their next trip should be to Charleston, South Carolina, where his other great-grandfather migrated to the states on a slave ship from Africa. And then to Jamaica where Marletta's family originated.

They are scheduled on a return flight back home to Indiana, flying out late Tuesday afternoon after they attend the Peace Corps meeting. It is scheduled for 9 a.m. in the beautiful World Trade Center on Sept. 11.

September 2000. Middleburg, Indiana

TEDDY

I open my eyes before the alarm goes off. It's the first day of my junior year at Middleburg High School. I remember my first school day a year ago when my body was in Indiana, but my heart was still in Arizona. The heart that was broken when Dad died. Mom decided to move us all—my little sisters and me—across the country to live in the house my dad had grown up in.

I lie here thinking, *This year will be different.*

Different because I can find my classroom on the first day without a cheat-sheet map in my back pocket.

Different because I know the names of my friends. Different because I *have* friends.

Different because I won't be sitting at a table by myself in the lunchroom, my only companion the humongous sandwich Baba makes that resembles the Subway party platter. Baba is my grandmother who we live with. The kitchen is her domain, and she thinks food solves all problems. Her kitchen smells good all the time.

Then the realization sinks in that although many things will be different and better, one thing remains the same.

Dad is still dead. Sadness creeps into my pores like a sponge soaking up a spill.

MARY

"She said she needs to sell or close the bookstore." I catch myself picking at my cuticles, something I haven't done for a long time.

I'm having lunch with my best friend, Rosetta, on the day Dianne, owner of A Good Bookstore where I work, tells me of her future plans. Her news makes me sad and I don't realize how much until the tears come as I repeat Dianne's words to Rosetta.

I go on. "What if no one buys it? It would be like losing the soul of the community. It's the heart of Main Street. Or what if someone buys it who cares more about the bottom line than the people? What if they bring their own staff and I'm not needed? What if…."

Rosetta puts her hands up, palms facing me. "Whoa, Mary, slow down. You're imagining all the worse scenarios. I'm sure anyone who bought a bookstore would have your same feelings about the connection between books and people."

I know she's right. "I guess I am being overly dramatic, but with so many changes in my life this past year, I just want something I love to stay the same."

Rosetta knows about the changes. The loss of my husband, Stan, in a car accident, a car my son Teddy was driving. Then a move across the country. Teddy starting a new school. My being a single parent. And the big one—discovering that Stan and Rosetta were high-school sweethearts, a forbidden interracial romance in the sixties that resulted in a son—Luther. A son Stan never knew of.

I'm still amazed some days that Rosetta and I evolved into friends through our twisted and shared history, yet I am so thankful for her.

Now Rosetta, always pragmatic, says, "There is another solution besides no store or grumpy new owner." She takes a sip of her coffee and peers at me above the cup.

I search for a tissue in my purse. "What?"

When I glance up at her, she is smiling. "Simple. Why don't *you* buy the bookstore?"

"Me?" I ask as if she suggested jumping off the Brooklyn Bridge.

"Yes, you. You've learned the business. You're looking for a career. Cathy will be in school full-time. Baba is always home for the kids. It's an ideal situation."

"I don't have that kind of money," I say.

"There are such things as small business loans, you know. And perhaps I'm being too nosy, but didn't Stan have life insurance?"

"That's for college. For all three of them, if I can stretch it that far."

"I see," Rosetta says. "Well, it's a thought."

She doesn't say anything more about it, and I don't either. When we part, we hug as usual, but as she breaks away, she puts both hands on my shoulders and looks me square in the eye. "Think about what I said, Mary. It might be a solution for the bookstore and Main Street, but most importantly for you. Doing something you care about. Giving you that purpose I imagine you're looking for." She gives me a quizzical look, and then adds, "Besides being a great mom, of course."

Two days later, she calls and invites me to her home for dinner. Her husband, James, is cooking as usual, and the enticing aroma of roasted chicken greets me at the door.

I yell into the kitchen. "I smell comfort food. Please tell me you have mashed potatoes too. But I'm staying even if you don't," I add quickly.

"Actually, red roasted," James says as I walk into the kitchen. He lifts the lid of the blue speckled roasting pan he has pulled out of the oven. Nestled among the pieces of crispy roast chicken are little red potatoes sizzling in the chicken juices.

"We'll let this rest while we have a glass of wine."

"How do you get the skin so crispy?" I ask as I peer into the pan and inhale the rich goodness.

"It's the blue pan." He gestures toward it. "Anything roasted should be in this blue speckled pan. Don't ask me why, but I am sure there is a good scientific explanation for it. Seriously." He nods to affirm this as he puts the lid back on. "Although I read in my *Cooking Light* magazine that a cookie sheet with a rim is best for getting crispy baked chicken."

I smile to think that this big, burly African American guy, who looks like he played in the NFL, subscribes to a cooking magazine.

The kitchen table is set for three. Rosetta hands me a glass of Riesling, my favorite. She says, "I thought the kitchen was cozier than the big dining room table."

"And we want to have a cozy conversation with you," James says as he pours a red for himself and Rosetta.

He sits across from her. "Mary, we'll get right to the point. Rosetta told me about the bookstore being for sale or closing, and we have talked about it seriously. If you would consider buying it, we would like to be partners with you. Silent ones, so to speak. You would have control of running the store. We trust your judgement and love your strong work ethic. It could be a good investment."

I have taken a sip of wine and almost choke on his statement. I swallow and pull in a big breath. "I don't know what to say. Why would you do this? Isn't it risky? Aren't there better places to invest your money with a greater return? I'm not sure how profitable a bookstore is." All these questions pour out of me, as if I'm thinking out loud.

Rosetta's brown hand covers my white one resting on the table. "Mary, slow down. It's an idea. Not a given. We'd like to see the books from Dianne, and of course, it would depend on what they show. If it looks good, it's something we might consider investing in. Perhaps we should have voiced it that way." She gives James a look that says, *I told you to go easy.*

I breathe a sigh of relief and take another sip of wine. "Maybe I need something stronger than wine," I say and we all laugh. "I'm not in the house five minutes, and you whisk the rug out from under me."

"Well, we thought it was not no so much a rug but a security blanket." Rosetta says. "Let's have our salads and mull it over." She heads to the refrigerator and pulls out a tray with three small salad bowls. "I'm trying to duplicate the salad we had the other day in Indianapolis. Romaine, walnuts, green apple, gorgonzola crumbles and poppy seed dressing."

James takes a bite. "You did it, honey. Good copycat."

"Delicious," I agree. "I love all the crunchy stuff."

No one speaks for a few minute as we enjoy our salads. Then James puts his fork down and looks at me. "You know I've spent most of my career in financial planning and I was just saying the other day that I'd like to explore something different as an investment."

"Bookstores are different all right," I chime in. "Not huge margins."

Rosetta says, "If this appeals to you at all, Mary, let's take the next step. Set up a meeting with Dianne for us go over her books for the last five years. What is her asking price? What are her terms? Then we can decide if it's something we even want to consider further. How does that sound?"

"This is exactly the right blend of flavors," I say as I take the last bite of my salad. They are waiting for an answer that I can't avoid. "I'd like that. Very much. And I should say thank you for your faith in me. That I could run a successful business. It's rude of me not to have said that right away, but I am a little overwhelmed."

"Of course," James says as he takes our empty salad plates to the sink and pulls a large serving platter off the top shelf. He carefully lifts the chicken pieces out of the blue roasting pan into the center of the plate. He places the red roasted potatoes around the meat. With a baster he extracts the extra juices in the pan and pours some over the entire serving platter. It's like a watching a maestro at work.

James places the platter in the center of the table. "Aside from the business details, what piques my interest is how Rosetta describes your enthusiasm for the business. For the store itself. I'm impressed with the projects you've initiated and put on the store's calendar as weekly events. The bedtime stories where kids come in their pajamas, the author signings you've snagged from writers who wouldn't normally come to Middleburg, enticing them with a guaranteed audience of their fans. The quarterly newsletter, especially the column where you encourage your customers to talk about their favorite books and authors. This type of community involvement makes for a successful business."

Rosetta chimes in. "And how many book discussion groups are there? Even a discussion group strictly for guys? What's it called? Real Men Do Eat Quiche? The Saturday Singles Group, your Teen Club. You're doing it all anyway, Mary. Why not reap the profits?"

"It's fun because now I don't have to worry about profits," I say as I take a bite of the moist and tender chicken. I chew and swallow the savory goodness. "I'll tell you what the bookstore needs. An adjoining café with your cooking, James."

"Or Baba's pizza," Rosetta pipes in.

"That's a great idea," I say. "No one can resist her deep-dish sausage. Actually, I haven't resisted anything she's cooked since we moved in with her. I've gained at least eight pounds."

Rosetta is kind enough not to say that I could stand to gain a few more. Food had no appeal to me when I was grieving for Stan.

"See, we're brainstorming already," Rosetta says. "I have a good feeling about this. I could work one evening a week. How fun to chat with the customers. Conscious people. As you can imagine, a surgical nurse doesn't have patients who are good conversationalists. That anesthetic can put such a damper on things.

James raises his wine glass, and we follow and clink. "To a good bookstore," he says.

Rosetta says, "It's good now, but it will be even better."

I raise my glass again and say, "To a better bookstore."

***

A month later, we stand back across the street so we can see from a distance the new sign that has been placed above the store.

A Better Book Store glows in bold green letters against a cream background.

TEDDY

Joe and I are having a Saturday burger at our favorite hangout—the corner drugstore with the 1950's red vinyl stools. They could have filmed *Happy Days* here. Nothing seems to have changed. Not even the burgers, making them the way I imagine they did back in the day. Definitely not fast food, as we watch Harry throw the fresh ground beef patties on the grill after we order.

"Nothing premade or frozen." Harry tells us each time he fries one up.

While the burgers are sizzling and revving up our taste buds, Harry starts on our milkshakes. He scoops in the ice cream, winks at me and gives me an extra dollop. "That one's for your dad, Teddy. We were in the same class, you know. He went on to college and I stayed here to help my family run the drugstore. Your dad never got uppity like some of those college boys did when they came in here on their school breaks."

I don't know if Harry forgets that he has told me this many times, but I don't mind hearing what a nice guy my dad was over and over.

A group of teens squeeze into one of the booths and feed the jukebox. Harry still has some of the fifties' music, and Bill Haley's "Rock Around the Clock" is blasting out.

Joe seems preoccupied. When Harry slides the finished plates to us with a dramatic flourish, Joe doesn't devour his burger the way he usually does, like a street sweeper after a monsoon storm in the desert. In fact, he pushes his plate away before every French fry is gone. Now I know something is wrong.

"So, what's up?" I ask.

"Huh?" he asks as if he just now notices I am there.

"If you don't finish your fries, there is a problem."

"It's Mindy."

"Oh, saving them for her? She would polish them off no doubt."

Mindy is barely five feet tall but eats like a sumo wrestler. She's been the love of Joe's life for a year, ever since I took her to his hospital room to tutor him while he was recovering from burns on most of his body.

"No, it's not Mindy. It's me."

"Isn't that what people say when they're about to break up with someone? It's not you, it's me."

Joe stares at me like I solved the mystery of the universe. "That's exactly the problem. I should break up with Mindy, and I don't know how. I don't want to hurt her, but I'm not being fair."

"Fair?" This comes as news to me. "What's happening? I thought you guys were doing great." His statement causes me to hold a French fry in mid-air.

I remember the day I introduced them and the spark that ignited between them. And how I decided I might have to squelch the attraction I felt for Mindy. Joe, I figured, needed her more than I did, missing so much school while in the burn unit. I also read Mindy's face as a subliminal message. She gazed at him like some kind of science hero because he attempted to build a rocket—the back-fired missile that resulted in his burns.

Mindy told me she was so in awe of the Rocket Boys after watching *October Sky* that Joe's failed attempt did not diminish his standing in her eyes. She was at his bedside constantly tutoring him with her quirky recollection of every fact in the universe. As their perfect fit became more apparent, I began to pride myself on making the introduction. To think of them not being together is puzzling to me now, as well as wounding my matchmaking pride a bit.

Joe pushes the rest of his fries toward me with a nod, giving me consent to finish them. He says, "Remember when I got back from Camp Courage in Arizona at the end of the summer? I told you how awesome it was to be surrounded by other kids with burns. How we didn't have to be self-conscious when we went swimming? Showing scars normally hidden by clothes? And we could all understand how hard it was to face the world with our disfigurements?"

"Yeah," I nodded, still not connecting this with Mindy.

"There was a girl. There *is* a girl. Tara. She lives in Nebraska, but was at the Arizona camp. Her burns were worse than mine, and she refused to leave the house although the doctor said there was no longer chance of infection. So Camp Courage demanded all *her* courage even to show up."

Joe smiles dreamily. "We got to be friends and I discovered that while I was trying to boost her morale, I seemed to forget about my own insecurities. By the end of the first week, I felt like some kind of superhero...well, maybe the way Mindy felt around me...like I was doing something good for someone."

Joe looks at me to see if I understand. I feel the need to respond, so I utter a meaningful phrase, "And?"

He goes on. "Tara and I have been emailing since camp, and I can't wait for her emails every day. Do you know the meaning of the name Tara?" he asks, his eyes lighting up.

Of course not. How would I know that? I shake my head, "No."

He sighs. "It's Irish and means Goddess of the Sea. Fits her perfectly because she swims like a fish. Said she feels free under the water where her scars don't show."

Oh boy. Joe's got it bad. I can see it in his eyes when he says her name. They light up with that same hopeful expression he had the first time I saw him at the hospital. Ours was a chance meeting one night not long after we moved to Indiana. I got lost in a hospital corridor after a minor biking incident that led me to the emergency room.

I turned a corner and found Joe sitting in his wheelchair. All wrapped in white gauze, yet his deep blue eyes had a spark that somehow conveyed hope to me. It's what made me go back to visit him and begin our friendship at a time we both desperately needed one. His buddies were busy with school stuff, and I didn't have any friends yet. I was the new kid on the block— the kid still mad at Mom for making me start over in a new school.

He says, "I feel like I'm being unfaithful to Mindy. Even though they're only emails, they make me feel so good. Like I can't wait to see her again, although who knows when that will be? She's a thousand miles away."

"So, you don't think you can be friends with both of them?" I ask, although I know the answer, especially if his feelings for Tara are more than friendship.

Joe shakes his head. "Get real, man."

"Okay, okay. I admit that was stupid."

"I would miss Mindy so much if we didn't talk every day, but it would be wrong to let her think she's the most important girl to me right now, because ...well, because she isn't."

"Could you tell her how you feel about Tara and how it happened and see what she says? I mean you didn't go to Camp Courage looking for a girlfriend. Seems it was innocent enough."

Obviously that was my second stupid question by the next look Joe gives me. "You've known Mindy longer than I have. What do you think she would do? Or say?"

"I've only known her about two months longer than you have. Sure, she was my friend first and to be honest, Joe..." I hesitate. Should I tell him how I feel about Mindy? "I never told you this, but I was starting to have some sweet feelings about her when I introduced her to you."

"Get out, man." Joe's eyes widen. "And you never told me?"

"She didn't have a clue and, frankly, I barely did either, so when the two of you hit it off, it was like the perfect match. And I still had her friendship and yours."

"Which might be more than I have if I tell her. I don't think that 'can we still be friends?' thing ever works. It doesn't in the movies. Since Mindy is the first girl I had a crush on, how would I know?"

"Me neither, man. We're both on rocky ground here. I don't even have *one* crush under my belt. The first kiss of my life with Elizabeth back in Arizona hardly qualifies."

"Oh my gosh, if you and Mindy got together, I would feel so good." Joe's face lights up like he has found the elusive missing piece in a puzzle spread out on the dining room table.

"Hold on here, buddy. I'll be a shoulder for Mindy to cry on, but I resolved in my mind that she and I would be just friends once you two connected."

Joe looks sheepish. "You're right. I can't pass her off like a used car. I'll figure it out. But I feel better now that I've talked to you. Maybe that's the first step."

When I drop Joe off at his house, he punches my shoulder. "Thanks, Teddy."

"I wasn't much help, I'm afraid."

Violetta Armour

"Yeah, you listened. You didn't call me a two-faced scoundrel."

"Because you aren't. If you were, you would string them both along and not even worry about Mindy's feelings."

Driving back home, I picture Mindy's sweet little face, her freckles, her purple rim glasses, her red corkscrew hair, and those turquoise braces. *How long is she going to wear them anyway?* So upbeat and energetic in her quirky way. I was already hurting for her and possibly the end of her fairy-tale romance. She was about to take a fall like Humpty Dumpty, and I wasn't sure I could put all the pieces back together.

I'm at a stoplight on the corner of 3rd and Lincoln. I pass it often and read the billboard on the Baptist church front lawn. They have an inspirational saying each week. "Some people come into your life as blessings, others as lessons." I wonder if Mindy was a blessing or a lesson for Joe. Maybe both?

I miss reading the quotes in the *Book of Life*, the book I found in Baba's attic that my great-grandfather brought through Ellis Island from Bulgaria. The quotes were such a crutch to me last year, missing Dad, trying to find my way in a new school. I guess I could read them again, but it wouldn't be the same.

I could write my own Book of Life. *Teddy's Thoughts*. But who cares about my thoughts besides me? *Teddy's Truths*? Now at age seventeen, what *is* true to me? Maybe someday my son will read them like I read my great-great grandfather's book. But what do I have to say that's so profound it would survive the ages?

Before the light turns green, three little kids hold hands as they walk. They keep rotating their positions so a different one is in the middle. One complains, "But you *always* get the middle. It's my turn."

A life observation and truth. Three is a hard number, and I am reminded once again of my talk with Joe. Joe, Mindy and Tara. Yes, three is a hard number in many ways.

Rosetta

"So what's bothering you?" James asks, as he reaches across the table and envelops both my hands in his large ones, his dark skin such a contrast to my mocha.

"What makes you think I am bothered?" I ask somewhat defensively. James and I are lingering over our last sip of wine before we clear the table. I keep flattening the edge of the placemat around my plate.

"You always do that placemat thing—like you're ironing it—when you have something important to say."

"Goodness, have we been married that long? Next thing you know, you'll be finishing my sentences."

"Something at work?"

"No. Work is good. It's about my parents. I'm feeling the need to tell them that Luther has a brother and sisters. They know Mary through the bookstore, but they don't know about our shared history. I don't know how much longer my mother has, and I don't want any regrets after she's gone. My dad said that her white blood count was up again."

"I couldn't agree more," James says. "Let's make a plan." He comes to my side of the table and pulls me up to embrace me in one of his big bear hugs. His arms almost wrap around me twice like a soft comforter.

I love this gentle giant of a man.

Before I fall asleep, I recall the day I told my parents I was pregnant. It was the summer after my senior year in '69. I never even told them Stan's name. What was the point? Simply that he was white, a naïve boy who would have insisted on getting married had I told him I was pregnant. An interracial marriage in the late sixties? Preposterous. What kind of struggles would we have encountered? Dad was more understanding than

Mom at the time. She was so angry that I sacrificed my dream of being a doctor, following in Dad's footsteps. I regretted it too, but now I wouldn't give up having Luther for anything.

Because Mom's cancer has returned with a vengeance, Dad tells me we might lose her soon. I keep telling myself that doctors are often wrong. How does anyone know how long a patient has? You hear stories all the time about people given a three-month death sentence, so they go on the cruise they've always dreamed of, and when they return they are in remission and live for many more years. But Mom is too weak for a cruise, and I fear Dad may be right.

That's why Mom deserves to know the rest of the story. And have a chance to meet Teddy so she can see what a young Stan looked like when he captured my heart so many years ago.

TEDDY

Mindy calls me. "Teddy, please come over. I need to talk to someone…no, not any someone. I need you."

I can tell she's been crying, and I know then that Joe has told her.

I couldn't refuse Mindy anything. She was the first friend I made in Middleburg. But she was more than a friend. After Dad died she was the one who made me laugh. She was the one who made me believe all my feelings hadn't died with him. That it was okay to laugh again even though I missed him.

"Be right there," I say with all the enthusiasm I can fake because I dread our conversation.

I haven't thought in headlines for a while, like I used to last year when the car accident made the front page news in Phoenix and traumatized me somehow. *Father Killed in Son's Driving Lesson.* Now a headline pops into my head for the conversation ahead of me. HEADLINE: *Fake It till You Make It.*

She's waiting for me on her front porch where we had countless conversations our sophomore year. Her nose is red and her eyes are puffy. *How long has she been crying?*

I ask, "What happened?" Even though I know, I can't admit that Joe had talked to me about it already.

She sniffles and says, "When Joe said 'we had to talk' I thought it was about the test coming up in English Lit. I grabbed all the class notes and my own study notes. I was so prepared. But I wasn't the least bit ready for what Joe said. How I wish it had been about Shakespeare instead of us."

Then in true Mindy style, even in her sadness, she analyzes things. "Well, in a way it was like Shakespeare 'cause didn't he always write above love? There's Rosalind and Orlando in *As You Like It,* Claudio and Hero in *Much Ado about Nothing* and the obvious *Romeo and Juliet*. Star-crossed, that's what I am now. Or more like *Taming of the Shrew* with unrequited love."

She wipes her nose with her sweatshirt sleeve, which like most of her clothes, is an eye-blinding color and oversized for her pint-sized frame. "Joe falls in love with someone at Burn Camp, and now I feel like the one who's burned. Teddy, it hurts so much. What's the name of that stupid camp anyway? Camp Courage. I could sure use some courage now.

"Joe said, 'Mindy, this is so hard for me, but I need to say this. I'm not being fair to you.' Then he put his head in his hands and I think I heard a sob…or at least a sniffle. That was my first sign that this wasn't about a Shakespeare tragedy. It was going to be *my* tragedy.

"But I couldn't face that thought, so I acted like it was about school. I said to him, 'Joe, the test won't be hard. We'll get through it with flying colors.'"

She goes on between sobs. "In spite of my phony positive words, I could feel my eyes watering and I didn't want to cry in front of him. Somehow I knew this was hurting him, too, because Joe's not a creepy, selfish guy. He's been through so much and he's sensitive to others' feelings. I guess you don't spend four months in a burn unit with surgeries and scars without a lot of empathy."

She shakes her head with a puzzled expression. "That's probably why I love him. And I want to keep on loving him. I guess I can. It's just that he isn't going to love me in turn." She puts her face in her hands and muffles another sob.

I don't know what to say. I put my arm around her shoulder and say, "Mindy, I'm so sorry. So sorry. I wish I could make it better." My comment, although sincere, sounds lame and not enough. Another headline coming on. HEADLINE: *Dear Abby. Where Are You When I Need Lovelorn Advice?*

MARY

I'm working the afternoon shift at the bookstore when the little boy sets the latest edition of *Goosebumps* on the counter. He digs deep into his jean pocket and pulls out three crumpled dollars and a quarter.

"Is it enough?" he asks. His expression is a mix of hope and fear.

I ring up the sale and say, "Well, almost. You need forty-seven more cents. Is your mom in the store?"

"No, she's next door at the grocery. She said I could come down here to get my *Goosebumps*." His eyes are pleading. "I've been waiting for this one a long time."

The man next in line behind the little boy slides two quarters toward me on the counter.

"Here you go, son." He is wearing a navy-blue tee shirt with a firehouse logo on it.

The boy looks up at me to see if I would approve this.

I nod, ring up the sale, and wonder if I should give the three cents' change to the boy or the man, but there isn't time to worry about it.

The boy grabs his book and takes off. As he goes out the door, he says over his shoulder, "Thank you, Mister."

"That was kind of you," I say to the fireman.

"Would never interfere with a good bedtime story," he says as he places his book on the counter.

"I'm not so sure it's good for bedtime. To hear some of the mothers, those scary stories keep the kids up at night. But the moms are so happy that their sons are lost in a book for the first time that they don't care."

I start to ring up his sale, *How to Cook Everything Vegetarian* by Bittman. "I thought firemen loved chili cook-offs and the more meat the better."

"We have a few guys at the house who are health-conscious. Trying to give them some options. My turn to cook tomorrow."

"Did you see the other one on that shelf? *Simple Vegetarian Pleasures* by Lemlen? I have a customer who says it's a good one. About half the price too."

"I like this one. Lots of pictures. Don't they say we eat with our eyes first?"

"We do." I agree and then offer, "I have a great veggie lasagna recipe. Even meat lovers like it."

"If you keep talking, I'm not going to have to buy anything," he says.

I smile. "You should get something for your two quarters."

"Seeing that kid's face was reward enough. But I have a feeling he was going to get the book whether I was here or not."

I hold up my hands, palms out. "Okay, you've got my number. But don't spread the word. Every kid on the block will expect it."

I slide a notepad toward him. "Seriously, I'd be glad to email you the lasagna recipe. I promise not to clutter your mailbox with jokes. Or perhaps you're in our database already?" I turn to the computer keyboard.

"I doubt it. Recently transferred to Station 43. My first time here."

I say, "Those guys at 43 are great. They helped us with a fundraiser last year to send my son's friend to a burn camp."

As he slides the note paper back to me, I notice he has no wedding ring. *A nice guy like that not married?* I feel myself blushing as if he can read my thought.

I am still wearing my wedding ring. Didn't seem to be any reason to take it off when Stan died. It feels good to have a little piece of him still with me.

Looking at his scribbles on the note paper, I ask, "Is it Mike?"

He nods. "Mike Santini."

"I'm Mary. So glad you came in."

"Me too," he says as he slides the dollars across the counter and peers at me with enticing dark brown eyes.

I feel a little flutter in my chest, but calmly ask as I hand him his change, "Need a bag?"

"Nope, headed back to the station and going to dig right into this."

After he leaves, I twist my wedding ring around on my finger. Rosetta said to me only last week. "You know, Mary, that wedding ring might discourage a potential suitor. It wouldn't hurt to have lunch or a date with someone."

I told her I wasn't ready. Not interested. But those dark brown eyes of Mike's were nice. And so was he. Paying for the *Goosebumps*, cooking veggies for his co-workers.

It was the first time I had taken notice of any man since Stan died. It felt both nice and a little bit not-so-nice.

TEDDY

I'm worried about Mindy. She hasn't called me in a few days. I go to her house on Saturday and her mother leads me to the family room where Mindy sits surrounded by books. I can hardly see her behind the stack.

It's two in the afternoon and she's still in her pajamas although she looks like she hasn't slept in days. Her curly red hair is going every which way and she has big dark circles under her eyes. I don't make any mention of this but try to act like everything is normal.

"Hey," I say. "I haven't seen you around school. Have you been going?" *Not like the brain child to miss a single day.* Last year we were locker partners and saw each other each day.

"Yeah, but not hanging around after. I have a lot to do here." She points to the stack of books and also has her laptop set up nearby.

"Uh, like what exactly do you have to do….here?" I also point to the books.

"Teddy, the Jeopardy Teen Tournament finals are coming up. I have to be prepared."

Of course, she would want not only to be prepared but over-prepared. "I can't even imagine where you would begin. I mean you don't have a clue what the categories are going to be."

She gives me a look of exasperation. "Exactly my point. I have to know *everything.*"

"Uh huh." I say as if knowing *everything* would be something any average person could do.

But Mindy isn't average.

"Could you take like a ten-minute break and talk to me? Or better yet, how about we walk to Patriot Park. Like we used to do on Saturdays. Isn't fresh air a good thing for those little grey cells of yours?" I tap my head. I'm secretly thinking a good shampoo might also be a plus today.

She looks at me as if I suggested going over Niagara Falls in a barrel. "Teddy…"she sighs.

"Okay. We can talk here. I'm worried about you. Ever since your breakup with Joe, you…you…I don't know. Maybe it's hurting you more than you realize. Would it help if you talked about it?"

"This isn't about Joe." Her eyes tear up as she tries to blatantly lie. "It's about getting back to what I do best and that's *being smart*. No one can take that away from me. It was silly of me to think I could be like normal girls and have a boyfriend too."

"Mindy, that wasn't silly at all. Of course, you can have a boyfriend. Joe proved that and there's probably other guys who might prove it too. But you'll never meet one if you don't leave the house."

"Not exactly true, ole boy. I met someone online. He's a fellow Brainiac."

"Really? How did that happen?"

"How did he become a Brainiac? Who knows?"

"I mean how did you *meet* him?"

There's this website called "Weird and Amazing Strange facts". You know how much I like that kind of stuff. And there's a place where people can comment and I did. It was about symbiotic-versus-parasitic relationships."

I'm afraid she's going to try to explain that to me, but thank goodness she doesn't.

"He replied to my comment and so we went back and forth and after this happened several times, we exchanged our personal emails and now we email each other privately instead of talking in the group chatroom."

It's neat that Mindy has found a Brainiac soulmate, but there's a nagging doubt in my mind. "What else do you know about him? Where does he live? How old is he? I don't mean to put a damper on your new friendship, but what if he's also strange and weird like the website? Like maybe a serial killer or something?"

Mindy laughs and I can't believe how good it feels to see her eyes light up the way they used to.

"Teddy, you sound like my dad. Like an old-man worrywart. And by the way, my parents don't know about this, so please don't say anything."

"If it's all so normal, then why can't they know?"

"'Cause they're parents, stupid." Mindy reaches for a book in one of her stacks. "It was nice of you to come by, Teddy. But now I have to get back to this. Today I'm memorizing all the capitals of European countries. Go ahead, ask me one."

My mind goes blank. I can't even think of a European country at the moment let alone a capital.

"I'm probably not the best study partner, Mindy."

"Speaking of study partners, I have a good one. Dr. Stone, Rosetta's dad, is going to help me with science and medicine. I'm going there tomorrow for a session."

"Now that's awesome, studying with someone you know." I say and I mean it. "Okay, I'll leave, but promise you'll call me if you want to talk or ...or anything. Remember how you were always there for me when I first moved here. I want to be here for you now."

"Aw, that is so sweet." She jumps up and gives me a hug. Up close her mouth smells like dog breath, and I'm thinking that besides a shampoo, she could use a toothbrush.

She walks me to the front door and before I leave, I say, "So what's his name?"

"Who?" she asks.

"Your new pen-pal. Mystery man."

"I don't know his real name. He calls himself "Lucky.""

"Does he know where you live?"

"No, mostly we talk about weird stuff...not normal stuff."

"Uh, huh, well, please keep it weird and don't give out any personal information, okay?"

"Geez, now you're the one being weird."

I leave thinking this *Mr. Lucky* might be someone trying to get *lucky* with a sweet innocent like Mindy. He's already lucky that he can't smell her doggie breath online.

MARY

The children come straggling into the bookstore in their jammies for Friday night bedtime stories. Some are carrying pillows, stuffed animals, and some dragging their favorite blankee. Mindy, who is the reader tonight, loves acting out the parts and changing voices for the different characters. She has an elephant-trumpet sound down perfectly.

The floor of the children's section is covered with quilts and blankets and curled up in one corner is Footnote, a large grey Maine Coon cat with bright green eyes. Some parents sit with their children. Others use this time to browse for their favorites in mystery, romance, and biography.

Because it is an evening event the hospitality table serves wine as well as the usual tea and coffee. Teddy sits at the table to ensure that only adults have the wine, after an incident where three freshmen downed an entire bottle of Chardonnay before teetering out of the store giggling hysterically. There's juice and cookies for the children. Crackers and cheese for the adults.

I love greeting the children and parents who have become regulars as they parade past me at the cash register on their way in. A little girl in Cinderella pajamas, who I don't recognize, stands hesitantly at the door and then is led with gentle encouragement from a man who holds her hand. He's wearing, of all things, Superman pajamas. But even more impressive than the big yellow and red S on his chest are familiar dark brown eyes. The eyes that made me wonder if Rosetta was indeed right in saying, "Maybe time to take that wedding off, girl?" I feel guilty at the thought of it as if I were being unfaithful to Stan to even consider such a thing.

"Hi Superman," I say. "Are you Cinderella's escort tonight?"

Violetta Armour

"Absolutely. Have to make sure she gets home by midnight… and hangs on to that glass slipper." He bends down to straighten her tiara.

"How did the veggie cookbook work out?"

"Good. And thanks for your email with the lasagna recipe. Haven't tried it yet and not sure I responded to you. Too busy with 911 responses."

I look at the pint-size Cinderella. "Does Cinderella have another name?" I ask.

"Do you want to tell this nice lady your real name?"

Cinderella shakes her head "No."

I say, "That's okay. Have fun and be sure to get a cookie before you leave."

The mention of a cookie appears to give me some credibility, and she rewards me with a shy smile.

As they walk to the children's room, I feel a stab of disappointment. Last week he wasn't wearing a wedding ring and now he has a daughter? A niece? Not hardly. I mean, would an uncle make the effort to wear pajamas? Again, a pang of guilt surfaces and makes me think of Stan. The fireman was the first sign of interest, although fleeting, I've had in the opposite sex. Is it too soon?

After story time, I remain at the checkout register when Superman comes with Cinderella toting three books close to her princess chest. When she reaches up and places them on the counter, I say to him, "I put you in the database last week, but you'll have to refresh my memory on your last name." I am glad no one is in line behind him so we can chat a bit.

"You mean it's not under Superman?" he asks with a smile.

"Should I look under Clark Kent," I say, feeling quite clever at my quick response.

He smiles. "Is there a phone booth here I can squeeze into to change?"

"Is there a phone booth anywhere these days?" I ask.

"Try Mike Santini," he says.

"Of course, there you are," I say as I tap the computer keys. "Would you like me to add your wife and daughter's name?"

"This is Jessica," he says, patting her head. "And I'll let my wife…ex-wife…create her own account. This is my weekend with Jessica."

Inwardly, I am embarrassed at my relief, which in turn makes me feel bad because divorce is not a good thing for anyone, and how sad that he possibly only sees this precious little girl on weekends. No wonder he's putting forth the extra effort.

"Well, she's a lucky little girl to have a daddy who is such a good sport. You're the first dad to come in jammies."

"Is there a prize for that?" he asks.

I smile with a nod at Jessica. "You have your reward. She looks at you like you are truly a superhero."

"I'm trying," he says and I sense a sadness that makes me want to reach out to him.

In an attempt to sympathize, I say, "I imagine it's not easy. I've been a single parent for a few years now. My Cathy is about Jessica's age. I wonder how long she'll remember her dad." This personal admission startles me as it spills out.

"Her dad's gone?" he asks with what seems like genuine concern.

"Yes, an accident."

"I'm so sorry."

"Me too." I almost tell him I bought the bookstore to give myself some sort of purpose again, but it's too much information. As Teddy would say, "TMI, Mom."

A few people have gotten in the checkout line, and the hour is getting late. I have to end this conversation although I don't want to.

He also seems to sense the waiting line and says, "Thanks. I'll be back."

As Mindy and I close up shop, she's putting books away and I'm running the day's receipts. I find myself hoping Mike Santini will come back soon as he said.

Mindy grabs her backpack from under the counter. "Kids Corner is back in shape. I put dry food out for Footnote and cleaned the litter box."

Our bookstore kitty, Footnote, is curled up in the earthenware bowl he likes to sleep in by the front door.

Mindy says, "It was a good turn out tonight. Did you hear all the giggling?"

"Yes, what were you reading?"

"Nothing that funny. Everyone was laughing when I wasn't even at the funny part. Then I saw Footnote burrowing under the blankets like a mole. He stole the show."

"Did I ever tell you about the night we had adult book discussion, and he weaved between the chairs and people's ankles. Then he poked his nose in one of the purses sitting open on the floor beside a chair. You know a cat can't resist peeking into anything that is open. He poked and pawed in the purse, and pulled out a five-dollar bill in his mouth. Walked away haughtily."

"Really?"

"The funny part was that she had a lot of loose singles in there too, but he picked the five-dollar one."

"Catnip can be costly, you know." Mindy slings her backpack over her shoulders and yells to the used book corner. "Good-night, Teddy."

Teddy yells back, "See you later."

Then to me, Mindy says, "Hey, did you see the dad who came in his Superman pajamas? How cute was that? He sat cross-legged with his daughter in his lap the whole time and he was hugging her like he never wanted to let go. I liked him."

Although I didn't say it, I thought, "Me too, Mindy. Me too."

TEDDY

I've been going to George's house about once a week 'cause I miss the weekly talks we had at the cemetery. Not much for a caretaker to do there all winter. I still visit Dad's grave, but it's not every Saturday like I did the first year.

I never thought one of my best friends would be in his eighties, but he tells the best stories. Some about being a Marine in WWII and a lot about growing up on a ranch in Colorado. Reminds of The Waltons re-runs on TV.

When I ran into George at the mall last Christmas, he said he was going to buy himself a computer. I saw it as a great chance to keep seeing him so I offered to help set it up. He liked that.

The first thing we do is create passwords. I ask him to choose one and write it down in the little notebook he has on his desk. His first choice is *cowboy*.

The computer responds: *Password must be more than eight characters with no blank spaces and contain at least one upper and one lower case letter and one special character.*

George looks puzzled. He says, "Special character? Well, I knew a couple of them on the ranch. Am I supposed to put his name in there?"

"No, just some kind of punctuation mark will do."

"Okay, I'll say *cowboy* ? I'm thinking of Dale who always had us scratching our heads. We never could figure that guy out."

He starts to write that down when I say, "Let's put a capital letter on Cowboy and take out the space between the y and the question mark."

George types that in and gets the special message about passwords again.

"Oops," I say. "I think we need one more to make it eight characters."

"So," he says, "Let me get this right. We need eight cowboys and one of them has to be special."

I laugh again. "Let's type in Cowboys with a capital C and put the question mark behind Cowboys with no spaces."

George talks as he types. "I don't know about this, Teddy. I thought this computer was supposed to make my life easier but so far it's kind of complicated."

"It will get easier. I promise."

We set up an email account for him, and he calls his granddaughter in California to get her email address. He sends his first email successfully and she responds with, "Grandpa, you are so cool."

She attaches a photo to her email which impresses George and me too. Makes me think I should keep her email address too. But I'm not into a long-distance romance. Last year I kept running to the computer after school to see if there was an email from my Arizona friends, Elizabeth or Wally. Most days I was sad when I didn't have any and sadder when I did if they described the fun they were having without me. I'm trying hard to make a life here with real friends instead of virtual ones.

Baba always sends food with me for George. When he came to the house last New Year's Eve for our party, she said he was way too skinny. Baba's mission in life is to feed the world. She must have taken that saying on the Statue of Liberty to heart when she came through. *Give me your hungry*...or something like that. Today we both enjoy her apple strudel.

There's a few birds perched on the bird feeder out his kitchen window.

George sets down his coffee cup and says, "Did I tell you about the time my brother and I killed the pet parakeet?"

"Nope." I settle back into George's comfy sofa, ready for another tale of his days on the ranch.

"Our youngest brother, Henry, had a snooty girlfriend who brought her parakeet to the ranch when she came to visit one weekend. Her name was Cheryl. The girlfriend, not the parakeet. The parakeet was Petey. No one in the family cared much for Cheryl. She was a city girl from Denver and put on airs like she was better than us country folks in the western hills of Colorado. Henry met her when he won first place in the bareback competition in the Denver rodeo. Of course, all the city girls liked us cowboys."

George smiles like he's enjoying a special memory.

"Well, Cheryl carried the damn parakeet everywhere she went, and I swear the parakeet had an attitude too. On this particular Saturday, Henry and Cheryl went to the barn dance in the schoolhouse gym, and my brother Dean and I stayed home on the porch trading lies and having a few beers. And babysitting the bird. We thought he looked a little thirsty, so we offered him some beer in a spoon through his cage.

I'm laughing already. "You spoon-fed beer to a bird?"

"Yep, by golly, he acted like it tasted good, so we gave him some more and he was chirping like he was a canary. After a while, Dean and I got to talking, not paying attention to the warbling. Then it was awful quiet. Poor Petey was lying on the floor of the cage with his feathers all ruffled and feet straight up."

George puts his hands up in the air, palms up. "He was obviously nursing a terrible hangover so we let him be. The next morning he was dead as a doornail, all curled up in his cage, and everyone was so puzzled as to what could have happened to Petey.

My brother Dean said with a perfect poker face, "Wow, that's weird 'cause last night we heard him singing his little feathers out—loud and clear."

I sort of snickered then, and I think Cheryl heard me. She never came back to the ranch, which made my parents happy. They couldn't imagine Cheryl being a rancher's wife and doing the chores in her fancy city clothes and hairdos. Nope, couldn't imagine her milking a cow or cleaning a horse stall with them pointy high-heel shoes sinking into the dung."

"Did you ever tell your brother what happened?"

"Don't recall that we did. But we figured we saved him a lot of grief. And some things are better left unsaid, wouldn't you say, Teddy?"

"I suppose," I say and dig into the apple strudel.

"Your Baba sure can cook," George says as he licks his fork clean. "Killing Petey wasn't nearly as bad as the time we thought we killed hundreds of baby chicks that came in a mail order. I'll save that one for next time."

I feel lucky to have old George around since I don't have a real grandfather. Uncle Dan is a good guy, always trying to fill in for Dad, but he's busy with his own family and job.

George has lots of time, and he's proving to me that family isn't always someone you're related to. It's someone you want to be with. Someone who's always happy to see you and you feel better when you leave than when you got there.

ROSETTA

James and I decide to have a dinner party with all the main characters in our family saga, or drama, whatever you call it. We were all together last New Year's Eve, so we think everyone knows each other. It might be good to refresh Mom's memory with faces, if I'm going to tell her the whole story.

We're using the guise of celebrating a successful month of sales at the bookstore, and that's not totally a guise as we certainly did. The dinner is at my parents' home, so if Mom gets tired she can go to bed. We invite the entire Kostoff family—Mary, Teddy, the little girls, Cathy and Ruby, and Baba. Luther and Marletta, and Teddy's friend Mindy, who adds a spark to any gathering. She and my dad have become great pals as she studies for her Jeopardy finals.

Then after everyone leaves, if it feels right, I will tell Mom and Dad, as Paul Harvey used to say, "the rest of the story."

Baba insists on contributing to the dinner, which usually means enough food for a Bulgarian wedding feast, but she loves doing it and who are we to deny her? Not to mention how good it all tastes. We're not stupid.

Baba arrives with a large pan of stuffed cabbage in a blue-speckled roasting pan. Teddy carries it in with two pot holders.

"Oh, this looks delicious," I say as I hand the pan off to James.

"James is the cook in this family," I say to Baba as he sets the pan on the stove top. James takes off the lid and inhales deeply at the bounty. "This looks and smells delicious."

Then he walks to Baba and gives her a hug. "I can tell we are going to get along great, Mrs. Kostoff, because I, too, am a firm believer in the blue-speckled roasting pan."

For a moment, Baba looks confused, then understands what he is saying. "Ya, the blue pan is the best. And please, you call me Baba too. Like blue pan, it is more friendly than Mrs. Kostoff."

She smiles and her hazel eyes light up between the wrinkles. Familiar hazel eyes I once loved in her son, Stan.

Luther approaches Teddy with a fist bump. "Teddy, good to see you, man."

I glance at Teddy, and the familiar lump forms in my throat as it always does when I see him. It's Stan. All over again. Young handsome Stan.

Teddy nods hello to my mother and reaches out to shake my dad's hand. "Hello, Dr. Stone."

My dad says, "Luther has told us all about you, young man."

Teddy glances at Luther as if to ask, "Why?"

Luther says, "My grandfather loves basketball. Comes to all the games so he knows most of the players by name."

As Teddy casually slides onto the high-top stool at the kitchen counter, I am transported back to the first day of senior year, when Stan slid into the high stool next to mine in the chemistry lab. And so it began. Now here we are, our lives joined forever.

My memory is disrupted when I hear laughter as Mindy comes in wearing a clown costume.

Teddy jumps off the stool and goes to peek under her mask.

"Mindy, did your invitation say, 'costume party'?"

"Let's be clear on this, Theodore. This is not a costume. It is my new work apparel."

"Oh, you work for Barnum and Bailey now? I didn't think the circus came to town until August." Teddy squeezes her big red nose. "What, no squeaker?"

"And that is the first misconception we learned at Clown School. All noses don't squeak."

"And all clowns are not funny," Teddy says. "Kids are terrified of them these days. Do you actually want to go around terrorizing rug rats?"

Luther says, "I've been leery of them since that Stephen King mini-series aired—what—about ten years ago? *IT.* And I was already in my twenties. Downright creepy." He turns to Mindy, "But surely you'd be one of those happy clowns at kids' birthdays?"

"That's what I was thinking," she answers. With her bright red hair she certainly doesn't need a clown wig.

"Clown school? Really?" Teddy asks with a chuckle.

"Yes, I am going to a one-week crash program at the rec center."

While all eyes are focused on Mindy, I walk by James and whisper, "I told you she livens up a gathering."

"Would you please pass these appetizers?" I say as I hand Mary a tray. "James, please offer our guests some liquid refreshment."

"Of course. Baba, what would you like to drink. We have coffee, ice tea, a Coca Cola?"

"Do you have any whiskey?" Baba asks. When James suppresses a smile, she adds, "For my arthritis, you know. The doctor says I should have a little whiskey each day."

Mary and Teddy roll their eyes at each other, and I smile at Baba's candor. Then I recall what Mary once told me. No filter.

Dr. Stone pipes in, "I'm sure that's good advice. Same advice I gave many of my patients."

"So you are doctor too? That is good profession. You still doctor?"

"I'm retired. I had a practice in Chicago, but I worked at the auto assembly plant here in Middleburg when it first opened. 1968."

Baba's eyes light up. "Maybe you knew my dear husband, Milan. He worked there many years. He was so proud. He write to his cousins in Bulgaria and say he has important job. Building American cars. It was maybe fender. No, the bumper." She frowns slightly. "I don't know what part, but it was important piece of the car. But he did not drive one. Someone told him, 'if you drink, don't drive.' Milan said he liked whiskey more than driving." She laughs.

Luther laughs too and I see a look on his face I had not seen before. Contentment? He's in the same room with both his grandmothers at the same time. He pulls Marletta closer to him as if to share this moment with her. He told me he confided his true heritage after they married.

As we have done so many times, Mary and I exchange a private smile. And I am thinking it's time other moments should be shared. Baba deserves to know she has another grandson.

ROSETTA

When everyone leaves, James and I start to clean up the kitchen, but he scoots me out saying, "Your mother looks tired. If you're going to talk to her, you should do it now before she turns in."

I agree and peel off the plastic gloves I had just put on to hand wash the big platters. "I was wondering if I should have asked Luther to stay with me but I think, for now, this is a conversation between me and my parents."

"Trust your heart," James says as he starts loading the dishwasher and I walk to the living room.

Mom is heading toward her bedroom but turns when she sees me. "Rosetta, this was a lovely evening, but I'm going to turn in if you don't mind."

"Mom, before you do, can we have a moment? You and Dad and I?"

She looks tired, but gracious as always, turns and says, "Perhaps a moment."

She sits back down next to Dad, close to him and he takes her hand in his. I'm wondering how many more nights he can hold her hand, and I feel a sadness for the loneliness he might soon experience. I sit across from them in the wing chair where Dad reads his medical journals, a whole stack of them spilling out of the basket beside his chair. Normally in perfect order, it tells me he is spending more time with Mom than usual. His normal routine is disrupted these days.

I don't have much time, but want to ease into the conversation. "So, did you enjoy meeting my friend Mary's family?"

Dad says, "That Baba, she's a hoot. Says whatever is on her mind. That's refreshing, isn't it? How old would you say she is?"

"Hmmm, my guess would be early eighties? But sharp as a tack, as they say. Mary says nothing slips by her."

He smiles. Mom looks sleepy. They wait for me to lead the conversation.

"Mom and Dad, one of the reasons I wanted you to meet Mary's family is because they are sort of my family too."

Again, Dr. Stone answers instead of her mother. "Yes, I can see you've become quite close. The bookstore and all. Glad it's going so well."

"It is good, Dad. But getting back to this family business. You see, not long after I met Mary, we discovered something we had in common—besides good books, that is."

"Oh?" my mother looks up. So frail that I wonder if I have chosen the right time. Perhaps a morning when she's rested would have been better, but I foolishly forge on, now anxious to get to the heart of the matter.

"See, what I found out, quite by accident, is that Mary, I might have told you, moved here from Arizona after her husband died in a car crash. To be with family."

"Yes, I recall that," Dr. Stone says. "Rosetta, your mother is tired. Should we continue this another time?"

"Please let me finish. I'll be quick. Mary's husband was Stan. And Stan was…" I take a deep breath. "…was the white boy I loved in high school." I watch their faces and it takes a minute for my words to sink in. To possibly understand what I am trying to tell them.

I repeat it. "Yes, Mary's husband was Stan and yes, he was Luther's father."

Is it my imagination or does Mom suddenly look even paler than before I told her?

Oh, my gosh, this wasn't a good idea.

"Oh, Rosetta," she says, and tears form as she tries to stifle a sob.

I look at Dad, fearful he will be angry that I have upset her. Was I way off base to share this now? Or ever?

"Mama, I'm sorry, I didn't mean to upset you. I thought …I thought you might want to know that Luther has a half-brother. One who looks exactly as Stan did."

"Rosetta, I am so tired. Too tired to take in your news. I need some time." She stands uncertainly, swaying a bit and takes a step toward the bedroom. My father takes her arm and walks beside her to steady her, but not before glaring at me in a way that says, 'Was this necessary?'

I return to the kitchen where James is still loading the dishwasher.

He looks up. "So how did…." but one look at my face tells it all. I reach for my half-full wine glass sitting on the center island.

"I guess this wasn't one of my better ideas. Bad timing." I say after I drink what is left in the glass.

"What happened? What did they say?"

"Nothing. Nothing. My mother said she needed to retire and my dad glared at me."

A few minutes later, my dad walks into the kitchen and comes directly to me. I brace myself for his scolding, but instead he wraps his arms around me and holds me for a moment. When he steps back, he takes my face in both his hands as he often does in a loving gesture and says, "My dear Rosetta."

My relief is so great I begin to cry. "Dad, I'm so sorry if I upset Mom. That was the last thing I'd want. Surely you know that."

"Of course I do. But why now, after all this time did you feel the need…"

I interrupt. "I don't want any regrets after she's gone. I thought it might give her some peace of mind that Luther could finally know who his father is, even though he could never meet him. And to know his heritage. And his other grandmother."

Dad says, "Speaking of Baba, I can use a shot of her whiskey about now." He reaches for the bottle of Black Velvet still on the counter.

"Allow me," says James as he gets a glass from the cupboard.

Dad sits down and takes a sip of his drink. He sets it down and shifts to look at me. "Rosetta, tell me how this remarkable story came about. You and Mary, now best of friends. How long have you known this?"

"About a year. I met Mary shortly after they moved here last September in time for the beginning of Teddy's sophomore year."

"And Luther? Does he know?"

"Yes, I told him last Christmas. Mary and I were going to tell both the boys, but then Mary decided it was too much for Teddy. Still grieving so much for his dad and all. Too much to take in."

"Well, I would say she was right about that. She's a good mother it appears."

"The best, in my opinion. To move across the country to spare Teddy from facing that awful intersection every day."

"The intersection?"

"I thought I told you. Teddy was driving the car when his dad died. It was an early driving lesson."

His face registers shock and anguish and then he says, "Yes, yes, I recall now that you did. Such a tragedy for that young man." Dad's genuine concern when he has so much on his mind now reminds me how sensitive my parents have always been to others' needs.

"Who else knows about this?" my father asks.

"Just Luther, Marletta, Mary and me. Mary wants to tell Teddy but is waiting for the right time. She says it never seems like the right time."

TEDDY

After dinner Mindy and I go back to her house to watch the closing ceremony of the 2000 Summer Olympics from Sydney. Sydney's summer, our winter.

Mindy explains, "The seasons in the Northern Hemisphere are the opposite of those in the Southern Hemisphere. Seasons occur because the earth is tilted on its axis relative to the orbital plane, the invisible flat disc where most objects in the solar system orbit the sun."

Mindy never misses a chance to spout her knowledge. It's probably one of the reasons she's not the most popular girl in school, but to me it's cute.

On TV, the commentators are raving about what an excellent host Sydney has been and how they've created a new standard of excellence for countries to follow. Actually, I could mute the sound since Mindy seems to know more about what's happening there than the announcers.

"I'm sure there will be an Olympic category at Jeopardy, so I am getting all the facts I can," Mindy says.

"But getting them and remembering them are two different things," I say. "Or they would be for me."

"So true. The weird facts are easiest to recall. For example, did you know the gold medals are actually made of silver—ninety-three percent?"

"So what are the silver ones made of? Bronze?" I ask.

Mindy laughs. "That I don't know."

"I don't think anyone should tell the gold medal winners they are getting silver," I say.

"That would be ninety-three US athletes we have to keep a secret from. We won the most gold followed by Russia and China." Mindy takes a bite of the brownies Baba sent home with us, but keeps on talking. "Now here's a fun fact. In the 1928 Olympics in Amsterdam, one of the rowers actually slowed down to let a little family of ducks pass. And he still won first place."

"See, his good karma paid off. Very ducky of him," I say.

Mindy throws a sofa pillow at me.

Although it goes way over my head, I catch it and throw it back.

"Good catch," she says. "You can qualify for the pillow-fight Olympics."

"No, some eight year-old would beat me out for sure. So what other Jeopardy categories are you going nutso over? Do you want me to quiz you while we watch these athletes celebrate?"

Her eyes light up. She loves to talk quiz. "Here's the latest category I am mastering. I'll give you a hint. There's over two hundred of them and we all have some."

"Two hundred? The first thing that comes to my mind is hair follicles."

She laughs and doubles over the pillow she is now hugging to her chest. "Do you honestly think hair follicles would be a category?"

"No, but...you have to admit some of the categories are so strange. Once I saw a category that was Chairs. What could be so interesting about chairs?" I ask.

Mindy doesn't have anything to say about chairs. Instead, "Here's the one that comes up quite often, so I'm memorizing a long list. It's Fears and Phobias. Yes, there's a word for over two hundred of them."

"My fear would be that I couldn't remember all of them," I say.

"There's even a word for fear of phobias. *Phobophobia*. There's a word for fear of body odor—*bromidrosiphobia*."

"Meaning a fear that you have it? Or that you'll sit next to someone in the movies who does? I'd go for a popcorn run and never return."

"My guess is a fear that you have it yourself. Not sure about that one."

She shrugs. "I'll never remember all of them, but here's what I discovered. All the words end in phobia. So you have to think, what would be a logical beginning of the word? Fear of air travel is *aerophobia*. Fear of animals is *zoophobia*, fear of loneliness is *autophobia*. See, auto means self. Loneliness means you are by yourself."

"But Mindy, you have to figure that out so fast. To be the first one who rings in."

"Yeah, that's a fear I do have and there's no name for it. That I'll

Violetta Armour

get one of those buzzers that don't work. You see it all the time—people clicking frantically and they can't get it to work."

"That would be *unclickaphobia*," I say.

Mindy laughs, throws me the pillow again. Although I do feel bad about her and Joe breaking up, I love spending more time with her again. Is there a word for fear of falling? I'm sure there is, but I don't mean the kind where you fall *off* something. More like you fall *into* something. Something like love?

MARY

To my knowledge and disappointment, Mike has not returned to the store recently. At least not while I'm working, which is pretty much all the time. Before Friday Bedtime Stories, I catch myself taking a few minutes to freshen my lipstick and eye shadow.

Silly of me to think he might have an interest in me. Who wants to date a widow who's still grieving? Barrel of laughs.

When I have pretty much given up on the notion that we might strike up a friendship, there he comes through the door. With two other firemen.

"Hey," he says. "My buddies and I were having lunch at the Mexican place on the corner, and I told them what a great little store you have here. Meet Todd and John."

"Hi, guys. And thank you… it's Mike, right?" I ask as if I didn't remember his name, although I checked the computer daily to see if he purchased something in my absence.

"You remembered," he says.

I feel myself blush and go back to the safe topic of restaurant talk. "You might also try Ming Lings next door to it. Great egg rolls." I smile at the three hunks in their dark blue tee-shirts with biceps bulging.

Mike says, "Todd needs some books for his wife. Chemo treatments. Four-hour sessions."

I gaze at Todd. "I'm sorry, but what a great gift idea. Do you know what she likes to read?"

"Hmmm… mostly mysteries."

"Come with me." I lead him to the mystery section and say, "There's a big variety. Cozy mysteries, true crime, suspense, British spy…"

Todd looks overwhelmed so I say, "Why don't I pick out a few of my favorite authors, and you can bring back any she doesn't like or perhaps has read."

He looks relieved as I pull a few from the shelf. An Agatha Christie, a Louise Penny, and a Mary Higgins Clark. "Here's one of the best…an oldie but goodie. *A Kiss Before Dying*. Made into a movie twice."

Mike has tagged along and says, "I told you she would be helpful." He heads toward the children's section. I am touched that he remembered me in a positive way.

I hand the books to Todd who continues to browse while I go to the children's section. Mike is crouched in front of the picture-book section.

"Have you been back to Bedtime Story Hour?" Why didn't I say, *I was hoping you would be back. I was looking for you and Cinderella.* That's what Rosetta, who thinks I should be dating by now, might have said in my place.

"No, I haven't had Jessica since the weekend I brought her in. It was supposed to be my weekend last Friday, but they made other plans."

I sense his disappointment and try to think of something kind to say when he continues, "We don't have a hard-and-fast rule about visitation. More of a verbal agreement. I try to be accommodating. It seems lately though that her mother is taking advantage of my flexibility."

Then he looks embarrassed as if he headed in a direction he didn't mean to. "Sorry, didn't mean to unload on you."

"Hey, anytime. Heaven knows I've been leaning on my friends this past year, burdening them with my roller-coaster grief. You think you're making some progress and then, out of the blue, something sad cuts you when you least expect it. Yesterday someone came in here who wore the same shaving lotion as Stan. I got one whiff and almost lost it." I feel myself blushing. "Now my turn to apologize," I say. "See, I didn't mean to say that either."

Mike doesn't respond but stares at me like he is concerned. Peering back into his warm brown eyes, I feel a little flutter in my chest like the first time I saw them.

Then he says, "Maybe we could have a cup of coffee sometime and both say all the things we don't think we should?"

"I'd like that."

I was hoping he would suggest a time and place, but he leaves with his buddies without doing so. Rosetta will not be happy about that, but they did buy six books, which will make James happy—more interested in the bottom line than my love life. Or lack of.

At closing time with no customers left in the store, I'm about to lock the door when I take one more stack of books from an end table to be re-shelved. When I hear a voice close behind me, I drop the entire armful.

"I didn't mean to scare you," Mike says as he leans down to pick up the books. "I was hoping you would still be here. Is it too late to have that cup of coffee…or even an adult beverage? I'm off duty until tomorrow night."

"I wish I could but afraid I'm on duty. I promised Cathy and Ruby I would read the final chapter in *Little House on the Prairie*. I said they could wait up for me tonight."

"Say Friday? How about lunch? I wouldn't mind trying that ding-a-ling place you said was good."

My disappointment turns to a laugh. "Ming Lings? That would work. I've got a helper coming in at 1:00."

He's still holding an armful of books. "You can set those down on this end table. I'll do them in the morning." I walk to the front door with him.

He pauses before going out as if he wants to say something else. Then simply, "See you Friday."

Driving home, I find it ironic that this evening's encounter with Mike happened the same way it did at first with Stan. Back in college. In a rainstorm. Me dropping my books, him picking them up. Remembering this makes me aware that I am comparing. Will I be thinking of Stan with each step?

I should cancel lunch. As nice as Mike is, I'm not ready—not even for nice.

TEDDY

The next time I go to Mindy's, her mother sends me to the basement. Have Mindy and her books been banished to the damp cellar? I can't imagine her doing anything bad enough to warrant any type of punishment from her lenient parents. They might reprimand her for reading at the dinner table or forcing the family to play with flash cards at meal time, but that's about it.

We didn't have a basement in Arizona, so I find them fascinating. Like an underworld sub culture, they're sort of like Baba's attic, filled with relics no longer useful, but maybe hold too many memories to part with. When we first moved in with Baba, I couldn't resist poking around in the boxes and dusty corners of the attic.

Mindy seems to be back to normal so possibly she's over Joe, but I'm still a little worried that I'll find her in the fetal position under a laundry sink nursing her broken heart—hiding from the cruel world that showed her love and then snatched it away.

Once she mumbled something about being better off before she met Joe. Said she didn't agree with Tennyson when he said, *Tis better to have loved and lost than never to have loved at all.*

But I find her perfectly upright, standing under a floor lamp shining on a long table full of stones. Smooth stones like river rocks. There are mason jars of paint with brushes in them—the kind we used to have in kindergarten on the easels. Primary colors. She is wearing paint-smeared bib overalls and sports a green smudge on her cheek. She doesn't see me at first, and I watch her. Is this some sort of art therapy for a broken heart, or is it a Jeopardy study project? Ancient Egyptian art? Hieroglyphics? I love her intensity and remember now why I was becoming attracted to her before she and Joe got together.

"Hey," I say and she startles.

She turns abruptly almost knocking over a jar of paint, then rights it. "Teddy. You scared me. Creeping up on me."

"Yeah, I'm a real scary guy." I put both hands up like claws and make a monster face.

She laughs, which makes me feel good. "I came to find out what you've been doing. Haven't talked to you much. Thought I'd see if you want to do one of our Saturday adventures. You know like we used to do?"

She glances at me with a little scowl. "Are you feeling sorry for me?"

I think she expects me to deny it or make some excuse. She seems surprised when I say, "Of course I am. I know what it's like to miss someone. It hurts and well… it hurts."

She doesn't say anything but picks up a stone and polishes it with a cloth. She's isn't going to talk about her feelings. I get that.

I ask, "So, is this a way to take your mind off Joe? Art therapy?"

She smiles and says, "Think fast." She throws me a stone. "I do have an idea for a fun Saturday project if you're game."

I catch the stone and say, "I'm in." I immediately have a twinge of regret. I should *never* commit to anything Mindy suggests until I get all the details.

"Do you know about the Painted Rock Project that has gone viral? It's sweeping the country."

"No, I haven't heard, but if it were actually sweeping, I might have heard of it."

"That's 'cause you probably live under a rock. Or a basketball," she scoffs.

I love that she's insulting me. This is the old Mindy. She's bouncing back. "Okay, so tell me what the whole world, except me, of course, knows."

"It's actually called the Kindness Rock Project. It started on a beach somewhere back east." Mindy dabs a bit of paint on a rock she has picked up. "Here's the story I heard. A lady walked the beach each day and picked up objects that reminded her of her parents who had recently died. Smooth stones for her dad, sea glass for her mom. One day she had a magic marker in her pocket and she wrote a message on one of the smooth rocks. *You are loved. You are special.* She did this on five rocks and left them on the beach.

"Later that day a girlfriend called and said she found a special rock on her beach walk. It blew the rock lady away that of all the zillions of rocks washed up on the beach, her friend would find one of the five she left.

"And what her friend said next changed everything. 'Well, I'd like to tell the person who left this rock that it made my day.' And that moment the Kindness Rock Project was launched. And now spreading across the country." She gives me a smug look like she just got an A on her oral book report.

She goes on in a rush without taking a breath like she always does when she's excited. "So I'm painting rocks and going to leave them in places around Middleburg. I hope someone finds them and it makes their day, then they will pay it forward and leave it for someone else, or better yet, plant their own rock with a special message."

Mindy's face is flushed and her freckles seem to pop off her cheeks. Then she smiles her goofy smile with the turquoise braces.

"Okay, I am definitely in," I say, as I grab a blue brush and a rock. "But one important question."

"What?" she asks in a curious and somewhat skeptical tone.

"Are those braces ever coming off or are you on the lifetime plan?"

Mindy laughs. "Actually, they come off next week. I can't wait to see if I have straight white teeth under them after all this time."

I write one word on my rock. "Smile."

Mindy looks at my word and says, "That's a good one. Hey, did you know that to smile you use seventeen facial muscles? To frown you use forty-two."

Of course I didn't, but I'm smiling inside and out to be with Mindy again.

TEDDY

When George says he should be writing down these stories he's telling me for his granddaughter in California, I show him how to create a word doc and then how to save it. When it asks for a name of the document, George thinks a minute and then he says, "I'm going to call it The Perfect Childhood. Because looking back, it sure was."

Once again, I think of John Boy and the Waltons and get comfy on the sofa.

George says, "Here's a story about my oldest brother, Slug. His real name was Leonard, but we called him Slug because one day he slugged the principal, old Waldo Runyard. Yep, he jumped across his desk and let him have it. Slugged him good—no one remembers why—and walked out of that schoolhouse and marched right down to the draft board. Of course, Slug wasn't old enough to enlist, but when the draft board called my dad to get his permission, Dad said, 'Go on, you can have him.'

"I guess Dad had gotten a call from the school and figured Slug would be better off punching out the Japs instead of school principals. Anyway, that's not the part of the story I want to tell you. That's just how Slug got his nickname."

"In my English class we call that the back story," I say.

George says, "So here's what I guess you would call the front story. After the war was over, Slug was in a group of American soldiers who were commissioned to round up all the horses in one section of France that belonged to the U. S. troops. He said it wasn't much fun telling a farmer who was now using the horse that he could no longer have him. But that's not the story either." George pauses and says, "What would your English teacher say about that?"

"She would call that extra material. Depending on the word count of the story or essay she wants, it might have to be left out."

"Well, you're getting a WWII story and I'm getting an English lesson."

"I like your part better. So what's the real story?"

"The real story is that the American soldiers rounding up the horses spent one night in an abandoned farmhouse, and down in the cellar, they found cases and cases of French champagne. Of course, they indulged in a few bottles of the bubbly. Not wanting the rest to go to waste, they loaded several bottles in the saddlebags of the horses being shipped back to America.

"One of the soldiers was a city slicker from New York. He had never ridden a horse before so he was skittish to begin with. As they rode through the French countryside, the sun came out and temperatures rose that summer day. Between the hot sun and the motion of the horses, the corks from the champagne started coming loose and soon all the bottles were popping like gunfire, shooting the champagne in every direction."

George laughs. "The loud bangs spooked the horses and they took off at a gallop. The poor city slicker from New York City fell off and swore he'd never get on another horse again. Slug said he said something like 'You can keep your damn horses. I'll ride the city subway any day.'"

"I'd like to go to New York City someday. Have you ever been?" I ask George.

"No, I haven't and probably won't. Awful crowded from pictures I've seen. I prefer wide-open spaces." George takes a sip of his coffee.

"How about champagne? Ever had that?" I ask.

"I believe we had a taste of that at your grandma's house on New Year's Eve."

"Oh yeah, we did. And I got to drink some too," I say.

"Taste good to you?" George asks.

"Not really. Besides I'm not much interested in drinking. Seeing as that's how my dad died. A drunk driver hit us."

"Sorry, Teddy, I shouldn't have brought that up," he says.

"That's okay. I can talk about it easier than I could last year. Still makes me sort of mad though."

"Sure it does." George scratches his head. "But if you ever get curious or want to see what all the fuss is about, come on over and we'll have a drink here in my living room. I'll pick you up and drive you home. Nice and safe here."

"Thanks, George," I say. "See you next week? Same time, same place?"

"You got it," he says as he slaps me on the back.

HEADLINE: *Teenager and Senior Citizen Tie One On.*

MARY

Rosetta, James and I meet once a week to talk about the progress of the store. I try to have a short written report of sales activity versus expenses and what is working well...and not so well. It's informal, usually over dinner, and I look forward to it each week, mainly to see what delicious concoction James has created in his man-kitchen.

"I met another man who cooks," I say as I marvel over James' braised short ribs with a deep-flavored sauce of onions, tomatoes, carrots and fragrant spices. He has removed the rib bones and sliced generous chunks of the meat into the sauce which he ladles over egg noodles. Rich and satisfying.

"Oh?" Rosetta says. "Do tell about the cooking man."

"I'll fill you in later with girl talk, after we go over the bookstore recap. I don't think James is interested in my man find."

"Didn't know you were looking," he says. "But I hope you are. You're still so young, Mary. You have a long life ahead of you. You need to share it with someone. I hope I'm not speaking out of turn....or too soon."

"Not at all. I appreciate your concern, and Rosetta's already on my case. I'm not what you might say looking, but this fireman walked into the store, wanting a cookbook for the firehouse and..."

"Let's finish up this book talk and get on to the good stuff," Rosetta's eyes are brimming with anticipation.

After dinner, Rosetta and I sit in her living room, the same room we first sat in before I knew she and my husband Stan were in love in high school. I peer once again at the painting on the wall of the pink rose bouquet with one red rose. I recall at that time the rose was one more clue that led me to think she and Stan might have been more than friends.

Someone, as in Rosetta, had left a similar bouquet at Stan's headstone, which seemed like a strange coincidence.

Rosetta fills our wine glasses and sits on the opposite corner of the sofa from me, her long shapely legs curled under her, shoes kicked off.

"Okay, tell me about this cookin' fireman. Is he cute?" Then she laughs. "Silly question. Aren't they all?"

"Yes, they are." I am drawing this out, knowing she is eager to hear more. "I wouldn't go so far as to say handsome. Maybe rugged—looks like he was in a couple of street fights as a kid, maybe even broke his nose at one time, but nice eyes. Brown. Warm."

"Mary, do you know this is the first time you've ever mentioned a guy? Is he the first who has caused you to take notice?"

"Yes. And to be honest I'm feeling a little guilty. Like it's too soon. Talking to him makes me feel alive. Is it all right to feel alive when Stan isn't?"

"Oh Mary." Rosetta leans closer and squeezes my shoulder. "James was right. You're young and pretty and deserve to be loved. Meeting someone else will never diminish what you felt for Stan."

I laugh. "I don't feel young or pretty. The problem is I don't feel much of anything. Doesn't seem fair to care for another man. Won't I always be comparing him to Stan?"

"That I can't answer. But I do know you won't know either until you try. What do you have to lose? Develop a friendship. See where it goes. I mean we're jumpin' the gun here, aren't we, thinking he's going to be your life partner 'cause you have a cup of coffee with him. Or one of those dinners from his new cookbook?" She gives me a mischievous smile.

"Oh, I'd have to go to the fire station to get one of those meals."

"Say, that could be fun. Slide down that fireman's pole. That would get his attention." Rosetta raises her eyebrows and smiles seductively.

I laugh. "Me? Pole dance? That's a good one." I pat her hand, which now rests on my knee. "I would never be so bold as to make the first move, but if he comes in again, I'll be as flirtatious as possible…whatever that means." I laugh. "Not sure I remember how to do that…or if I ever did."

I tell Rosetta the little I know of him and how sweet he was with his daughter. She jumps on that immediately. "Why not set up a playdate for her and Cathy…. meet at the playground?"

Violetta Armour

"No, no, no...that implies too much togetherness. I like the lunch idea for starters."

"Okay, then get started, girl, and keep me posted."

Later that evening I ponder again the strange twist of fate that has brought Rosetta and me together. Stan's high-school girlfriend in the sixties, a beautiful black girl who secretly gave birth to a son he never knew of, Luther. Now the varsity basketball coach whom Teddy admires, with no inkling that he is his half-brother. Someday I will have to tell him. At the right time.

How will I know when it's the right time?

TEDDY

The annual father-son banquet at school for all the athletes is coming up. This year the coaches decided to have two dinners. One at the beginning of the seasons to inspire anyone who was going out for sports, they said, and one at the end of the year to reward those who made it.

I ask Uncle Dan to go with me, but he has to be out of town that day. I've heard that the banquet is a lot of fun when they roast the coaches. And sometimes there's an inspirational speaker, usually one of our graduates who talks about how playing a sport changed his life in a positive way

When missing Dad is especially painful, I slip back into headline mode. HEADLINE: *Annual Father-Son Banquet at Middleburg High. Orphans Need Not Apply.*

The next day Coach Luther approaches me as I'm checking out the bulletin board outside the athletic office.

He points to the banquet poster. "Teddy, I've been thinking about the father-son dinner. Since neither of us—you and me, that is—have a father or a son, how about we pair up?"

"Don't you have to sit with all the coaches?"

"I'd rather sit with the players. Probably a lot more fun."

"What about Rosetta's dad? Or James? Don't grandfathers or stepdads count?"

"Oh, they count for a lot of things. And Grandpa loves sports, but he's curtailing his activities with my grandmother not doing so well. Hates to spend time away from her. Besides, I'd like to sit with you."

"I'd love to go with you, Coach. Thanks so much."

"Great!" he says. Then he stands there like he wants to say something else, but he doesn't.

I wait and then say, "We don't have to wear matching shirts or anything, do we?"

Coach laughs and slaps me on the back. "I hope not."

On the night of the banquet, they don't give out any awards because that comes at the end-of- the-year banquet.

Some of the seniors who got awards as juniors are asked to say a few words. Al Nedoff, who got the most valuable player football award last year says, "I know this is a father-son thing and my dad did teach me to throw a spiral, but my mom drove me to all the extra practices and always had a hot dinner ready if I missed one. I think the Moms deserve a special dinner too."

All the guys cheer and I can see why Al, besides being a good athlete, is also senior class president. He'll probably be voted "most likely to succeed" at graduation.

Nick Cain, a low handicap golfer, says his coach taught him to be happy for other players' success. "It's such an individual sport that sometimes we forget we are still a team."

Rodney Hanson says, "My mother said to be sure to thank the volunteers who did all the laundry. Uh, like all the wet towels we used at each swimming practice and meets."

Coach Duffy gets up to speak and everyone groans. I don't get it, but Luther whispers to me. "He goes on and on and it's a tradition that everyone razzes him about it. He's come to expect it and would be disappointed if it didn't happen."

I'm so glad Luther is here to fill me in.

Coach Duffy holds up his hand to stop the noise and says, "Most of you have heard the story of how our guy, Sam Reeves, overcame a bad fall to finish first in the high-hurdles event. For the division championship. In case you haven't, I'll remind you. Also, 'cause I love to tell this story." Coach loosens his tie like he needs space to breathe. The room is quiet now.

"Although there were six runners, everyone knew this race was going to be between Sam and Troy Froder from Terre Haute High. The gun goes off and sure enough, Sam and Troy take the lead quickly. But at the very first hurdle, Sam takes a fall and comes skidding down face first. A collective gasp sounds from the bleachers and then silence. Surely, the race is over for him. But Sam jumps up and keeps going. At lightning speed.

The crowd starts roaring and it keeps getting louder and louder as Sam is gaining. Just before the finish line, the sound of the crowd gets Troy's attention. He looks over his shoulder to see how close Sam is. Some say that look cost him. In that split second, Sam catches up to him and crosses the finish line by one second.

"An exciting finish to say the least, but what I wanted to point out to you tonight is that Sam didn't win that race when he crossed the finish line. Well, sure he did, but in my opinion, he won that race when he came in early before school every morning to practice. He won that race when he stayed later than anyone else after school to practice. He won that race when others said, 'Hey, let's go get a coke at Miller's drugs,' and he passed.

"What these exceptional athletes do is make the finish line look easy. The winning basket, the perfect pass or the catch in the end zone. They make it look easy because they have done it so many times *when they didn't need to do it.* I hope all of you tonight leave with this message—that you're willing to put in the hours it takes to make a champion."

Coach pauses and we think he's done. A few people clap, but he holds up his hand. We should know he isn't finished. He fiddles with the knot on his tie again like he isn't used to wearing one and then he says, "Now, everyone doesn't need or want to be a champion. Maybe you love the camaraderie that sports provide. Maybe you like riding on a team bus for hours or maybe you just want to wear a letter jacket that all the girls like." A few chuckles come from the crowd.

"That's okay. But remember your reward will equal the effort you put into it. And that's true of anything you're going to do with your life…your job, your relationships, your family.

I love working with you boys. Now let's dig in…pass those mashed potatoes and roast beef."

Now everyone claps.

After the banquet Luther gives me a ride home, and when we reach my house, I thank him again.

"It was something I wanted to do with you, Teddy. I might know a little bit about how you feel without a dad. See, I never knew my dad either."

"Never? Why not?" I ask, and then think that perhaps I'm being too nosy. "I'm sorry, I shouldn't have…"

"Hey, it's okay. I brought it up, and I don't mind talking about it. My mother got pregnant the summer after her senior year of high school. Right here in Middleburg actually."

"Here? I thought you grew up in Chicago."

"I did and I was born there, but I came back here to coach after college. There's nothing like Hoosier High School basketball as far as I'm concerned."

"Oh, you saw the movie too?" I ask. "Every basketball fan loves *Hoosiers*."

"Of course," he says.

When he doesn't say anything else, I ask, "Did your dad die too?"

Luther hesitates and then he doesn't exactly answer my question. "All I know, I mean *knew*, about my dad was that he was white. He and my mom fell in love. They had to keep it a secret." Luther turns away from me and stares out the window on his side.

Then he turns back to me. "You know from your U.S. history class that the sixties were a hotbed of racial tensions and unrest. There was no way my parents' relationship would have been accepted. In fact, the opposite; they would have been ostracized."

"So then what happened?" I ask.

"What happened was my mother and her family moved back to Chicago. Nine months later I was born."

"What about your dad? Did you ever get to see him?"

"That's the sad part. My mother never told him he had a son. Never even told him she was expecting a baby."

"That's crazy," I say, then quickly apologize. "No, I don't mean your mom was crazy. The situation was crazy. And sad. I mean I can understand why they couldn't get married, but wow…for him not to know."

"She said she was afraid he would insist on getting married. He was sort of an idealist who thought they could, as they say, 'beat the system'. Heck, it was only 1967 that interracial marriages were approved by the Supreme Court."

"So you never even knew his name?"

"No, but we had such a big family in Chicago. Trust me, I had a lot of father figures. Uncles, cousins, Grandpa Stone…"

"Now that you're older, would you like to find him? Not to stir up any trouble or anything. Aren't you curious to see him?"

"Sure. There were times I wondered. I used to look at my mom's senior yearbook and try to guess who it might have been. I never told my mom I did this. Didn't want to make her feel bad. She's been an awesome mom…still is."

"My mom showed me my dad's yearbook. It's still at Baba's house."

Luther clears his throat. "Hey, it's getting late and tomorrow's a school day—for both of us. Guess I shouldn't have rambled, but wanted you to know I understand how you must feel sometimes."

Mom's in bed when I come in, but her bedroom door is open and the light is on. I poke my head in. She's reading as usual.

"Good-night, Mom," I say.

She sets her book aside. "How was it?"

"Great. There were some funny roasts about the coaches. I'm glad I got to go because all the guys will be talking about it tomorrow."

"That was nice of Coach Luther to invite you."

"Yeah, he's a great guy. Did you know…"I start to say and then catch myself. Maybe Luther told me all this in confidence. Like he's trusting me with something special.

"Know what, honey?" she asks.

I quickly think of something else to say. "Did you know basketball tryouts are next week? I can't wait. Good-night, Mom."

"Night, Teddy." She puts her bookmark in place, yawns and turns off her reading lamp.

Before I fall asleep, I have a good feeling about the night. Being with someone at the banquet, especially Coach Luther. I think about his mother's story and then I wonder if she was in high school when my Dad was. I should get the yearbook out again.

Rosetta

When Luther swings by my house late on a school night, I suspect something is wrong, but when I see his face, I am relieved. He looks happy. Like after a basketball win.

"Hey, Mom, sorry to drop in so late. I saw your light on."

"You know you can pop in anytime, light or no light. You've been out?"

"Tonight was the father-son athletic banquet. I just dropped Teddy off."

"That's right. I knew that. How was it?"

"Good. But I came by to tell you about a conversation I had with Teddy. I probably should have cleared it with you first. I…"

"Did you tell…?" I feel a knot forming in my stomach.

"No, Mom, I would never do that without yours and Mary's blessing." I breathe a sigh of relief. "So what needs my approval?"

"I did tell him that I never knew my dad. That he was white. And… and that you got pregnant in high school. I hope that was okay."

"It's fine, Luther, but what prompted that conversation?"

"He kept thanking me for taking him, and I wanted him to know I could understand how he must feel sometimes without a dad." Luther's eyebrows furrow. "But wouldn't your pregnancy be your story to tell, not mine."

I quickly reassure him. "It's our story. And Teddy's story too. And one he needs to know."

"That's what I'm thinking too. Can we talk to Mary and see what she thinks? About when we might have this conversation with Teddy."

"Of course. I'll talk to her, unless you want to be with me when I do."

"Why don't you bring it up, but at some point I want to be in on it. It's important to me that we be honest with him. If I know, he should too."

"I agree, honey. I do."

"And there's one other thing." Luther gives me the smile that always tugs at my heart. The one he used as a toddler when asking for 'just one more cookie.'

"I genuinely like that kid. Fist bumps are fine, but lately so often, I want to hug the boy. Wish I could make some of his pain go away. I can't replace his dad, but some big-brother love might help."

MARY

I want to call Mike to cancel lunch but am not sure how to reach him. I can't make a personal call to the firehouse. It's probably his day off, and this is hardly a fire emergency. I check the database for a number but don't have one. I could say my one o'clock helper didn't come in. But what if he drops in anyway and sees that I'm not alone? No, can't get caught in a lie. No way to start a relationship. And who says it's a relationship yet? Oh, I might as well go. What's one lunch?

He orders beef and broccoli and I order cashew chicken and a pot of tea. He suggests that we share and I like that. This must be a new waitress because she leaves us fortune cookies as soon as we order instead of at the end of our meal.

Mike opens his. "We don't have to wait for dessert to eat these, do we? To discover our fortunes?" He raises his eyebrows as if we're onto something good here. He's like an eager kid, which is cute. He reads his and laughs, "It says, *Order take out. You will be hungry in two hours.*"

Opening mine, I read it silently. I recall the fortune cookie I got before we left Arizona. Something about *Start new life.* How my best friend Kate said I was nuts if I was moving a thousand miles away based on a fortune cookie. Those days are a blur now. I was so grief-stricken, so frightened and floundering, trying to do the right thing for the family. Sometimes when I remember the early days following Stan's passing, I feel the anxiety I did then. The constant butterflies. I don't remember how or when they began to subside.

Mike's voice startles me for a second. "Hello. Are you here? Was your fortune a bad one?"

"Oh, sorry, had a déjà vu moment. Actually, it's a good fortune. I read aloud a made-up one. *You will meet a handsome stranger.* I hear Rosetta's voice saying, *Be flirtatious.* So I surprise myself and say to him, "And I just did."

"Are you making that up?" he asks.

I laugh and push the little paper toward him, "Now, why would I do that?"

He reads it aloud. *Flattery will get you everywhere.*

"Everywhere? So where is it you would like to get?"

Is that a twinkle in his eye?

"Actually, I'm in a fairly good place right now. A minute ago, when I zoned out on you," I say apologetically, "I was recalling a fortune cookie a few years ago. Before I moved here and just after Stan passed away. I was so confused as to what to do. Coming to Middleburg proved to be a good thing, although at the time I had no idea if it was right or not."

"So you haven't been here that long? And already a pillar of the community?"

"I wouldn't exactly say pillar…"

"But surely, you know a bookstore can be the heart of a small community. The right kind of store, that is. And you have the right kind."

"That's nice of you. Now who is doing the flattery?"

"But I mean it…seriously."

Our food arrives and smells delicious. "I could eat Chinese every day," I say as I inhale the steamy goodness.

"Possibly you were a geisha girl in your former life," he says as he spoons some beef and broccoli onto my plate. "Remember, we're sharing."

I spoon out the cashew chicken for both of us and pour two cups of tea. We eat in silence for a moment. "You believe in former lives?" I ask.

"Hmmm. Not sure. Don't give it much thought, to be honest. Do you?" He asks, taking a bite of egg roll.

"I'm not sure either. I do wonder what happens after death more than I used to …with Stan passing so suddenly. It's all a mystery to me."

Mike pauses, puts his fork down, and gazes at me. "You know I wanted to say… any time you want to talk about your husband, I understand. In fact, I would welcome it. That you would trust me with your feelings would be a compliment."

"That's kind. And you can talk about your ex-wife too. Remember that was our agreement—to talk about whatever we didn't think we should."

He clears his throat. "For starters and in full disclosure, I should tell you she's not my ex-wife yet."

A piece of chicken feels stuck in my throat. *What is he saying? He's still married?*

I must have looked stricken because he reassures me. "All the papers have been signed. The court date is coming up. We need to resolve a few child-visitation issues. That's one reason I've been rather lax on our verbal agreements with Jessica. Don't want to antagonize the situation."

I picture his little Cinderella and I see concern in his eyes. "I understand. I hope it works out for you. She's a darling little girl."

"It's why I transferred to Station 43. To live near her mother." He pauses and then adds, "And her stepdad, Lance. Well, he isn't yet, but will be once we're divorced."

"Is he a good guy? Do you like him?"

"Seems nice enough. As long as he treats Jessica well. Had a few strikes against him to start as he was dating my wife while we were still married. They traveled together for business. A perfect setup for infidelity, I suppose."

Mike is so kind that I wonder why someone would stray from him, but I also know that every story has two sides. Or I've heard three sides. His, hers and the real story. I suppose whoever I meet at this stage in my life or theirs will have *baggage*.

"This food is good," he says. "Let's try the Mexican next time though."

He wants a next time? I do too, but is it to find out if his baggage is just a carry-on or the maximum fifty pounds the airline allows. *How much can I carry?*

TEDDY

Mom and I have started doing this corny thing at dinner. Something we used to do during dinner with the family in Phoenix. Dad started it, but when we came to Indiana, the rite was forgotten. Then we started again. Tonight Mom asks, "What's the best thing that happened to you today?"

Ruby and Cathy always have quick-and-easy answers. "It was my turn for show-n-tell," or "I got to use the easel. Teddy, look at the picture I made." Cathy points to her latest masterpiece on the fridge. Bold primary colors, a bright yellow sun in the top corner. A red A-frame house. Four stick figures holding hands.

Ruby says, "I'm teacher's helper this week," and continues to line up her tater tots in a row. She doesn't want them to touch the other food on her plate.

They look at me now. I can't think of anything to say. Not that my days are bad, but neither are they particularly exciting. Mom is always trying to keep things positive, so I go along as best I can. I say, "It might be fun…or more interesting…to tell the weirdest thing that happened. I'm sure there's more of that on some days."

Mom laughs, "Oh, you want weird. If this is a contest on who has the weirdest story, I win hands down. This lady came into the bookstore today. A good customer, Gertrude, who buys a lot of books. Hardbacks, new releases, so I'm always happy to see her."

"Mom…." I say, steering her back on track, knowing she can quickly digress to book titles, reviews and sometimes a plot or two.

"Okay, Gertrude walks right past the front register and motions for me to follow her. So I do, thinking she needs help finding a book. She keeps looking around to see if other customers are near us but it's mid-afternoon. All is quiet.

"She leads me to the biography and history section and pulls a little

Violetta Armour

blue ceramic pot out of her purse. Then she says, 'Mary, I don't know if I told you that my father passed away last month down in Florida, where he and Mom retired.' I try to express my condolences but can hardly get a word in as she keeps talking."

"'We had him cremated and one of his dying wishes was that we would put some of his ashes in a bookstore. He loved bookstores.' She raises the pot and says, 'So, do you mind if I leave him here on this shelf? Biographies were his favorite.' She smiles at me as she places it in an empty corner of the shelf, assuming I would approve. I mean, how could I refuse? Deny a dying man his last wish? And a booklover. What could it hurt?" I asked myself.

"So he's there on the biography shelf?"

"Yep, Mr. Sheldon Parks, right there with Truman, Jefferson, and John Adams."

"That's a good place for him 'cause aren't most of the people on that shelf also dead?" I say.

Mom smiles and tussles my hair.

"You're right, Mom. You get the prize for the weirdest day."

Cathy scrunches up her nose. "Ashes like from the fireplace. That's silly."

Then Mom glances at me and says, "Actually, Teddy, I should not have put that incident in the weird category. We should make a new category— what was the most loving thing you experienced today? I saw a lady who loved her father enough to honor his wishes."

Cathy says, "Can we have a fire tonight in the fireplace? And make s'mores?"

"Not tonight, honey." Mom gives me the eye roll that indicates we should change the subject.

"So, anything weird for you today?" she asks. "Since weird is your idea."

I could tell Mom about Patti—Patti with the pretty green eyes asking me to the Sadie Hawkins dance. I don't know if that would qualify as the best thing or the weirdest thing. Or both. Weird because she's the most popular girl in the junior class, so why would she ask me? And the best? Well, because she's the most popular girl.

HEADLINE: *New Kid in Town Gets Noticed.*

MARY

Our next meeting—*are these dates or meetings?*—is a lunch again, and as Mike suggested, we're at the Mexican restaurant. Between our two schedules, lunch has been a better time for us rather than evenings. The waiter brings the chips and two salsa bowls to the table, one mild and one fiery, as soon as we are seated.

"I love this stuff," Mike says. "The hotter the better," as he dips a chip into the fiery bowl.

"I'll have to bring you home sometime for Baba's cooking. She's from Bulgaria, and they love their hot peppers."

"So tell me about Baba. I assume she's a grandmother. Your mother?"

"No, Stan's mother. She came to America as a young girl. About sixteen, and her marriage with Papa…he's gone now…was arranged by two aunts. She said they spent about ten minutes in a room alone to get acquainted."

"I've heard of speed dating. Maybe that's the first instance of it?"

"Lasted forty-seven years until he died. He was quite a bit older than her."

"Did you have a chance to meet him?"

"Stan brought me home from college one weekend to meet his parents. His dad made his own wine and offered me a glass as soon as I walked in. Stan should have warned me that his "wine" was about 150-proof. About knocked my socks off."

"Where are your parents?" he asks.

"They died while I was in college, one shortly after the other. Stan's family is all I have now. No brothers or sisters. How about you?" I push the chips further away, so I'll stop munching.

"Big Italian family. Three crazy sisters. I love them, but I swear they're nuts. I don't think I could be married to any of them, although I love their passionate natures, but I fear for their husbands. No matter how much screaming and carrying on though, divorce is not an option in our family. They love as deeply as they find fault. So, I am the exception, but they're taking my side in this. It's a good thing they don't live in the same town as my wife. I'm not sure she would have survived their wrath." He munches on a tortilla chip.

I wait for him to chew, hoping he'll continue, enjoying his story.

He looks sheepish. "They're protective of me...all older. I was a late surprise to my parents when they thought their family was complete with three beautiful girls."

"So you were probably spoiled rotten?" I ask with a little grin.

"Of course. Still am. Whenever I feel a little low, I drive up to Chicago to get my fix. Great nieces and nephews too. Jessica is fascinated with her cousins, although at times she's overwhelmed by their—what shall I say—boisterousness? Kind of a carnival atmosphere. Bocci games on the lawn, everyone talking at once, my brothers-in-law arm wrestling, plenty of wine and big bowls of pasta coming out of a rambunctious kitchen."

"It sounds wonderful. I want to go to the carnival." I hear myself saying, which surprises me. I hope he knows I'm kidding. *But am I?*

"You'd get the third degree from my protectors. I wouldn't subject you to that."

Our food arrives with the usual warning, "Careful, the plates are hot."

"Is that phrase the first thing they teach new employees?" Mike asks after the waitress leaves.

"Hot salsa, hot plates, lots of hot going on here. But as a fireman I guess you can handle hot. What made you decide?"

"My dad. A fireman for forty years. In downtown Chicago. He's retired now but still claims his station was the original one that responded to the fire Mrs. O'Leary's cow supposedly started back in 1871."

"You actually know the year?" I ask surprised.

"Oh sure. Heard the legend many times. It was on a Sunday. South side of Chicago. And practically everything that could go wrong did. Firemen went to the wrong location." He laughs and says, "I'm a little surprised Dad admitted that. Fierce winds made the blaze jump the Chicago River twice. The Chicago Waterworks burned down, making it impossible to fight the fire. Finally, after two days Mother Nature took over and rain smoldered the flames."

"Wow," I say. "That's a great piece of history."

"There's so many stories I heard, hanging out at the station house after school and on weekends. All my friends thought Dad was cool, kind of a hero worship. And I loved the way the guys at the firehouse seemed like a family."

Mike's face takes on a glow when he talks about his sisters and now his father's firehouse. He seems like such a family man and I feel a sadness for him. "I'm sorry your marriage didn't work out."

"Yeah, and I wanted a big family. We got a late start. And now it looks like an early finish. Maybe I shouldn't have married a woman who traveled so much for work." He breaks up a tortilla chip and drops it on his plate as if he doesn't know what to do with his hands.

It seems he wants to take the spotlight off himself when he says, "So tell me about your kids."

I tell him about Teddy, Cathy and Ruby. About the car accident and our first year in Middleburg. "Looking back, I'm glad we made the move. Teddy has made friends and he's getting to play basketball again. Junior varsity, but hopefully varsity this year."

"And you?" he asks.

"If the kids are adjusting, then I'm happy. And of course, I love the bookstore. It's sort of like having another child. When I first took over, I could hardly be away from it for more than an hour. I would start getting anxious. Reminded me of when Teddy was born. I wanted some time alone, but couldn't stay away long."

"Sounds like we're both rebuilding our lives," he says. "Would you want to marry again?"

"Are you proposing to me?" I tease. "Gosh, we haven't even kissed."

He smiles. "Well, we should do something about that." He reaches across the table, takes my hand and gently places his lips on it.

Something inside me stirs. Something so tender. Something I haven't felt for a long time. Then I feel the tears blurring. I don't pull my hand away, but I look down. Not soon enough though, as Mike notices.

"I'm sorry…I didn't mean…"

I glance up and smile through the tears. "Please don't be sorry. That's the kindest thing anyone has done in a long time. My first kiss since Stan….and it was …it was just right."

TEDDY

The night of the Sadie Hawkins dance, I dress in Western clothes—a plaid shirt Mom bought me, Levi's and boots. I borrow a bolo tie and cowboy hat from ole cowboy George. He also loans me an awesome shiny Hesston belt buckle showing a cowboy with his hat and lariat. He polishes it for me and tells me it's part of his collection. He has one for every year from 1974 to 1988.

I'm totally into this now, and I feel like I should have a horse hitched up to the front railing. Instead, Patti and I ride in the back seat of an SUV that belongs to Brett's dad. We're double dating with Brett and Rachel.

This is my first date since I moved to Middleburg and I'm nervous. Last year Patti was the first girl I noticed in my Honors English class, but she was dating a senior on the football team. What chance would a lowly sophomore have?

Coach Luther and his wife Marletta, are chaperoning. When they have us pose for a picture in front of a giant display of hay bales, I notice Coach watching and smiling and then he gives me a thumbs-up sign. Somehow he always makes me feel better.

They try to teach us to square dance, which is sort of a train wreck. Got my "do-si-dos" and "swing your corner" a little mixed up. Instead I swing my partner and do-si to my corner and crash into three people on the way. We laugh so hard that someone cries, "Stop, I'm going to wet my pants."

At that command, everyone stops. It's like we're playing a game of statue. We all freeze except the poor girl who runs off to the restroom. Now I no longer have a corner to swing or a do-si to do. We laugh again as we walk back to the corner of the gym out of harm's way.

Then they play Aerosmith's "I Don't Want to Miss a Thing." Obviously, we're supposed to slow dance. Yikes. I shuffle my feet around, but not well, and when Patti suggests that we get some punch, I am relieved. Her toes probably thank me too.

As we sip our drinks, I survey the room and realize I know a lot more kids than I thought I did. Then I spot who's missing. My two best friends. Joe and Mindy. Joe is somewhere in virtual Nebraska with Tara, and Mindy is home alone, nursing a broken heart. Cramming for Jeopardy. Or she's online with that creepy Lucky guy.

Although I'm having a good time, and Patti is awfully cute in her western skirt with lots of petticoats—three, she told me—and a little red and white bandana around her neck, I wish I were with Mindy, making her laugh, helping her forget about Joe, and of course, taking her verbal abuse, which I have come to expect and enjoy.

HEADLINE: *Ranch hand Ted Looking for Brainy Cowgirl.*

TEDDY

I go to George's the next day to return the belt buckle from his collection before I misplace it.

He asks me about the dance and I ask him if he had a girlfriend in high school.

"Well, that's sort of a funny story. Not one but twelve."

"What?" I ask, totally surprised. "George, you've been holding out on me."

He laughs. "Not really girlfriends, but I did have twelve dates. When I was a junior, there were twelve girls in the senior class and only one boy, so I told him I would help him out in the dating department. I actually made a bet with my dad that I would date all twelve senior girls before the year was out."

"Did you do it?"

"Yes, I had a date with each one except Doc Zeigel's daughter, and the year was coming to a close. I finally told her about the bet I made with my dad and she said, 'Well, let's go to the picture show.' And we did." He says, "Now are you ready for the baby chick story?"

"Always ready for one of your stories." I help myself to a soda from his fridge, not so much for the soda but because he likes it when I make myself at home.

"At the ranch, we received a big mail order of a couple hundred baby chicks each spring. They always arrived when it was storming and cold because it was in March. We had a brooder house with lamps, but because we never knew exactly when the chicks would arrive, the heat lamps were not on. So Dad put them in our house around the heating stove in our parlor until the brooder house warmed up.

"We had all the baby chicks set up on newspapers close to the stove.

Dad told us kids to keep the fire going because he and Mom were going to town for supplies. Well, we sorta overdid our job with too many logs, 'cause the house got too hot and caused a globe fire extinguisher over the stove to explode."

"What's a globe fire extinguisher?"

"It did exactly what it's supposed to do when it gets too hot. It takes all the oxygen out of the air to stop a fire. But with no oxygen, soon all the baby chicks started falling over, dead as doornails. We knew we were in deep trouble. At least we thought so until we gathered up the dead chicks and took them out onto the front porch. Once they got a whiff of that fresh cold air, some of them started moving again. We got real busy taking them out and giving them all artificial respiration by pulling out and flapping their little wings. By golly, we saved them all. And saved our hides too."

It was sort of funny that this was the day Baba sent me with leftover fried chicken for George. Didn't curb our appetites any.

On the way home the church sign reads, *When it comes to friends, four quarters are better than a hundred pennies*. I'm thinking friend George is more like a silver dollar.

MARY

The next time Mike pops into the store, he's wearing his firehouse clothes so I assume he's on duty.

"Just have a few minutes," he says, "but I was wondering if you were free Saturday night? We've only met during the day, so I wasn't sure if you were allowed out after dark." He smiles. "Some kind of curfew?"

"Funny guy," I say.

"I'm off Saturday night and would like to cook dinner for you—one of my firehouse specials."

"At your house?" I ask. Then realize how silly that must sound.

"That's sort of what I had in mind. Unless you prefer the firehouse kitchen and sharing a table with five other guys."

I shake my head. "You know, this is all new to me. Been over twenty years since a guy asked me to his place. This *starting over* is weird."

He looks dejected.

I'm quick to say, "No, *you're* not weird. The situation…"

He interrupts, now with a small chuckle. "Hey, I get it. It's the same for me. Not twenty years but long enough. Didn't imagine I would be dating again."

"So is this a date?" I ask with a grin.

"If it's after dark it's a date," he says with mock seriousness.

"Then let's do it. Let's be bold and daring. What can I bring?"

"Your appetite," he says, as he glances at his watch. "I gotta run."

He heads out the door. I have no idea what time or where he lives.

Violetta Armour

TEDDY

The next day I head over to Mindy's, and no surprise—she's buried deep in her book cave. She looks up, doesn't say 'Hi' or shout out a greeting a normal person would. Instead as usual, a weird fact spills out of her mouth.

"Teddy, listen to this. If you add a pinch of salt to water when boiling eggs, the shells won't crack."

"And you need to know this because…? Do you really think eggs will be a Jeopardy category, or are you also auditioning for the Iron Chef?"

"Yesterday they had a category that was Hints from Heloise, so I'm checking those out. Here's a good one. Ants never cross a chalk line. So if you have an army of ants marching across your kitchen floor, get out your chalk and draw one."

"I'm going to have to test that one. Does it work on a picnic blanket too? Isn't that where they usually parade?"

"Good question. You're getting smarter just by hanging around me." She grins. "So how was the Sadie Hawkins dance? Did a lot of girls ask you to dance?"

"Nope, only Patti, the one I went with."

"Patti's cute," she says. I know Mindy well enough with her insecurities about her looks that she's probably thinking, *Patti's cute and I'm not.*

"She is cute… but you are too." I've never once said anything nice like that to Mindy about her appearance. Mostly I tease her about her braces or all the weird colors she wears.

Mindy looks at me with tears forming behind her purple glass frames. "Teddy, you don't have to be nice to me 'cause Joe found someone else."

"I wasn't being nice. I was being honest."

She acts flustered, and the spaces between her freckles turn pink as she blushes. "Let's get back to Heloise," she says. "Did you know that if you have a splinter, Scotch tape will pull it out better than a tweezer and won't hurt either?"

"Good to know," I say not wanting to make her feel uncomfortable any more.

"And that fizzy tablet for an upset stomach—*pop pop, fizz fizz*—can unclog a sink drain. Drop three tablets and follow with a cup of white vinegar. Wait a few minutes and run hot water."

"You know you're putting some poor plumber out of business with these old wives' tales." I pick up a stack of index cards with questions on them and ruffle them like a deck of cards.

"So what did you do last night? Go to a chat room with that Lucky guy?"

"Actually, I did. He told me about some websites that might have Jeopardy questions. And he sure asks a lot of questions."

"Like what?" I still have a queasy feeling about this guy.

"Mostly he wants to know what I like to do, my favorite movies, what books I'm reading. Stuff like that."

"Does he tell you his favorites?"

"No, he doesn't say much about himself. I guess 'cause I don't ask—maybe I should. That would be the polite thing, I suppose. What do you think?"

I don't tell her what I really think, which is, she shouldn't be giving out information to a stranger. But I want her to keep telling me about him, so instead I say, "That's nice that you found someone who might help you study." As if Mindy needs any help in that department.

She's back in Jeopardy mode. "And here's my favorite hint of the day. Put a miniature marshmallow in the bottom of an ice-cream cone and it will prevent melting ice cream from dripping out."

"Hey, great idea. Let's go to Millers' and get a sundae—like we used to after our Saturday hikes."

Mindy glances up at the clock on the wall and says, "Sorry, can't right now. Lucky said he would be online at two o'clock."

MARY

Rosetta and I are having a glass of wine after the store closes on Friday night. She's going to ask about Mike, and I'm eager to talk about him too.

She doesn't disappoint me. We barely take our first sips when she asks, "So how's your fireman?"

I feel myself blushing and say, "He's not *my* fireman."

"Okay, how's *the* fireman?"

"Oh, you mean Mike?" I ask, and we both laugh.

"Actually, he's good and I wanted to talk to you about him."

"I'm all ears, girlfriend. Tell me."

"Well, not so much him as the situation. Did I ever tell you about my dreams of Stan?"

"Hey, what happened to Mike?"

"It's all connected. Lately I've been having a lot of dreams about Stan. I didn't when he first passed. I'm sure I was still in shock back then."

Rosetta says, "I read something about the shock factor after a sudden loss. The denial part can even erase that person from our subconscious. It's too painful so we avoid it altogether."

"Yeah, I guess that could happen. At first, they were mostly happy dreams. He looked good and I usually felt content when I woke up. Other than missing him of course. Some nights I even looked forward to going to sleep, thinking we might have a little dream rendezvous."

Rosetta smiles.

"This one time though, it was so crazy. He was laid out on a table like he was sleeping, but I knew he was dead. His hands were placed one on top the other. All of a sudden, one hand started flopping around. In my dream I thought, 'Oh, that must be that *rigor mortis* they talk about.' I knew he would be embarrassed if people saw his hand doing that. Some people were milling about the room, but I'm not sure who they were. You know how weird dreams can be."

Rosetta nods.

"So I went over and put his hand back where it belonged, and then he sat up with a big smile and bright eyes and said, 'I'm fine. Everything is fine.' I think he meant, *fine, as in I'm alive again*. And here's the worst part." Now I cover my eyes and shake my head before I can continue with the dream story.

After a few seconds, I go on. "Instead of hugging him and saying, 'I'm so happy you're back,' I stood there frozen, thinking, 'Oh my gosh, how will I tell him he doesn't have a car anymore or clothes or his golf clubs.' As if those things were more important than him. As if those couldn't be replaced."

"Oh, Mary, I'm sorry."

"No, it's okay. It was strange but what I wanted to tell you is that since I've been seeing Mike, I have not dreamed about Stan. Not once. So, of course, I have to ask myself, 'What does *that* mean? Does he want to bow out now and let Mike in? Is he trying to tell me it's okay? Or is he angry with me? Is it too soon? Does he think I'm forgetting him?'"

"Of course he's not angry. He would want you to be happy. Surely you know that."

"And then I tell myself, 'if I have all these questions, it may be too soon. Not fair to Mike.'"

"Do you think about this when you're with Mike?"

I pause and think about it. "I don't think so. Mainly when I'm alone."

"Then how can it be unfair if it's taking nothing away from your time with him?"

I peer at Rosetta and know why I am so thankful she is my friend. I say, "There's a new book by Marlo Thomas called *The Right Words at the Right Time*. You could have written it. You always say the exact thing I need to hear at the time I need to hear it."

"That's me. Always dishing out advice even when no one wants it." She laughs. "The book sounds interesting though."

"I only glanced at it briefly, but perhaps the theme is that often a person tells us something we may not recognize at the time as having significance, but years later we recognize that their advice or praise is truly meaningful for our lives."

Rosetta's face lights up. "I know exactly what you mean. Like just yesterday. Don't know why, but I thought of something my grandmother said to me when I was pregnant with Luther. My friends were leaving for college—September, 1969. Grandma caught me crying in my room as my cousins came to say good-bye and drove off for their freshmen year. Although they were kind enough to suppress their eagerness, I watched from my window as they piled in the car full of joy and anticipation.

"I was having a real pity party, thinking of what I was missing—dorm life, football games, parties. Not to mention feeling stupid that I was responsible for the situation I had put myself in.

"My grandma sat beside me on the bed, put one arm around me and said, 'Your cousins are creating college memories. You, Rosetta, are creating a life.' And she patted what was starting to be my baby bump. Then she said, 'Years from now, which one do you think will be more important?'

"At the time I still wanted dorm life more than a baby. Hey, I was only eighteen, but now I look back and recognize her wisdom."

We ponder this thought as we sip our wine, and then Rosetta says, "Hey, we were supposed to talk about Mike. Tell me, tell me."

I tell about our lunches and all he told me about his family. She smiles and says, "Mary, your whole face lights up when you talk about him."

"It does?" I ask, somewhat surprised.

"Yes. And that's a good thing." She chuckles. "A very good thing."

I set my wine glass down on the table. "There is one problem."

"Oh?"

"His divorce is not final."

"Will it be soon?"

"So he says. Do you think I should wait until it is?"

Rosetta doesn't miss a beat. "To have lunches and be a friend? Probably exactly what he needs now." She pats my knee as if to give her blessing and approval.

I smile and recall his sweet kiss on my hand. *Maybe he's exactly what I need now too.*

TEDDY

It's cool having a part-time job at the bookstore. It beats standing over a greasy french-fry station at a fast-food joint. Although free fries would be a good thing.

Mom has put me in charge of the used-book corner, which is growing like crazy. Soon it's going to need more than a corner. People love bringing in their used books and knowing they can get credit for them. They don't get cash, just credit toward their next purchase. Most of the time, they seem satisfied. A few mumble that their book is worth more than we give them.

If it were me, I might say to them, "Why don't you just keep it if it's so valuable?" but I guess that's why I'm not the one dishing out the credit.

HEADLINE: *Avoid Teen Helper at Bookstore.*

Mom responds with tact as she explains how it works. That if we give a lot of credit, we have to charge more for the used book and people expect a real bargain when buying a used book....blah, blah, blah. They must accept that because they bring in a lot of books.

Then it's my job to take the used books out of the bags or boxes they drop off in my corner, organize and shelf them, and write the price on the inside of the front cover in pencil. Mom made a chart for me as a guideline, but I usually have to set aside a stack I'm not sure how to price.

Some days it takes me longer than others because I find myself starting to read them. And sometimes I find the most interesting things people leave in them, bookmarks or grocery lists or something they just plain forgot about.

Like today I find a twenty-dollar bill in the pages of a paperback. "Wow, my lucky day, since Mom only pays me minimum wage. Like when you find money in the pocket of a coat you haven't worn for a long time. *Bonanza.* Except the coat belonged to me and this book doesn't.

I carry the old khaki duffel bag that's about to fall apart to the front of the store where Mom is entering new titles into the computer inventory. "Mom, is the person who dropped this off still in the store?"

"He walked out a few minutes ago."

I run out and see someone about to get in a car, which looks as battered as the duffel bag. I'm thinking he can probably use the twenty.

"Hey, Mister," I call. "Did you bring some used books in to trade?" I hold up the bag.

He turns and says, "Yeah. What about it?" He sounds annoyed.

I wave both the book and the twenty-dollar bill and say, "I found this in...uh—" I glance at the title of the book, *Message to Garcia.* "Kind of a cool bookmark so I thought you might like to keep it."

He walks toward me, now smiling. "Hey, you're alright, kid." He points to the book. "Have you ever read this?"

"No."

"I thought you had because you're displaying the qualities it describes."

"Like honesty?"

"A little more than that. Have a look. It's a short read...about finding someone reliable who will get the job done...along those lines." He gingerly takes the twenty from my fingers and says, "Thanks, kid. I should go back in and tell the owner what a good employee you are."

I give a little laugh. "She'll agree with you, but she might be biased."

"Oh?"

"Well, Moms tend to think their own kids are great."

"For sure I'm going in now," he says and walks back to the store.

After he leaves Mom says, "I'm proud of you, Teddy."

"Well, you know, good karma and all. But it was tempting to keep it. With the paltry wage you pay me, I can hardly survive."

She taps me lightly on the head with the book in her hand.

MARY

Tonight is dinner at Mike's. I can't decide what to wear and change my clothes three times. I feel like a teenager. This is crazy. It's just a dinner. He has only seen me in the clothes I wear at the bookstore, so I want to jazz it up a bit without going overboard. I settle on a long denim skirt and white tee with some nice jewelry that I don't normally wear. Where's Rosetta when I need her? She told me once that after you put on all your jewelry, take one piece off. I remove the dangling hoop earrings that remind me of a Vegas call girl and put on the ordinary gold hoops I always wear. I leave the blue pendant on. A little more eye shadow than usual and a touch of color to my cheeks. I am so not confident.

As I leave my bedroom, I glance at the photo of Stan and me on the bureau. Smiling, happy, at the beach with the wind blowing my hair and my head back laughing. As if he's told me something funny like he usually did before someone snapped the photo. Something goofy like 'don't say cheese. Say wine…or better yet, say beer.'

I remember that day well. Each summer, we left the heat of the desert for a week in San Diego. Rented the same house on the beach. We would barely get in the door when the kids would strip off their clothes, grab their suits and run to the water's edge to dip their toes in until we could join them.

The first year we did the normal sightseeing in the area. Lego Land, the famous zoo, Sea World. The last few years we hung around the house and relaxed, watching the kids make sandcastles, building a fire on the beach at night to roast hot dogs and s'mores, watching the fireworks. Good memories. Is there a way to hold onto the good memories without letting them haunt me? I guess I'll find out soon enough.

I have butterflies as I a drive to Mike's, and my palms are sweaty on the steering wheel.

I find his home easily—a townhouse in a new development in town. I turn off the car and sit there. I'm a little early so I have time to stew. What's wrong with me? I'm putting way too much importance on a simple dinner.

I walk to the front door, but hesitate before I ring the doorbell. One deep breath.

Mike opens the door, wearing the equivalent of a man apron, a white towel tucked into his jeans. The place smells good—like Sunday-dinner pot roast. I recognize the music as a song from college days, *Good Morning Starshine*. It makes me feel good. I glance at the TV behind him on the wall and see that the station is set to the 70s Music Channel.

He gestures me in with the sweep of a hand. "Welcome to Mike's Diner."

"Pretty classy greeting for a diner," I say. "Don't they usually have a girl whizzing by on roller skates to steer you to the nearest red vinyl booth? Or that would be the fifties."

"No skates for me...that would be a wreck waiting to happen. Follow me please. Not that you could get lost in this expansive floorplan." He points to a narrow table in his small kitchen, now set with a checkered tablecloth and a little vase of pink carnations in the center.

"From your garden?" I ask.

He laughs. "I had one live plant in the window. It died a slow death. And we are eating on the only china I have. Well, china might be a stretch." He points to two plastic plates on the table. "I have two more that match, so three guests is the most I can have at one time." He winces as if to apologize. "This is, you know, a bachelor pad. And a meager one at that."

I glance around the small kitchen. "It's nice...it's cute...it's—" I try to think of something better to say. "It's homey for someone who just moved in."

"Yes, barely."

I smooth out a corner of the tablecloth. "Did you get this tablecloth especially for tonight?" I ask, thinking surely no man has a dowry of linens when he and his wife split up.

I detect a slight blush. "I wanted to make a good impression."

"You certainly have. It's charming. And something smells delicious."

"I didn't invite you to the firehouse kitchen, but we are having firehouse food. My specialty, other than my new vegetarian recipes, is pot roast in the crock pot."

"Old family recipe?" I ask.

"Sort of. But I had to call one of my sisters to ask about one ingredient—something about a bay leaf. I didn't have one and couldn't remember if it was important or not. She asked if firemen were that fussy, and I made the big mistake of saying, 'This is for a nice lady I invited to dinner.' Big mistake." He opens his arms wide "That means I'll be getting a call in the morning to see how it went."

"The pot roast or the lady?" I ask.

"Definitely the lady."

"Did she give you dating advice as well as cooking?"

"Not exactly. I guess you could call it advice, but more for you than me."

I laugh. "For me?"

"She said to tell you that if you didn't treat me nice, Cousin Vinnie would soon find you."

"I had every intention of being nice, but for sure I will now."

A kitchen timer dings and saves us from a conversation about the Chicago mafia.

As he unplugs the crockpot, I say, "Nice is not what she should be worrying about. Perhaps boring might be a better word."

"You, boring? I hardly think so. Why would you say that?"

"I should confess that I'm a little nervous. You'll recall that at one of our lunches I told you I haven't seen anyone since Stan died. And driving over here tonight, I wondered about what people talk about on dates these days."

Mike walks toward me slowly and takes both my hands in his. "I want you to be comfortable with me. Let's not call this a date. Let's say two friends are having dinner. How's that?"

"That's nice," I say.

He gives my hands a little squeeze before he lets go. The little squeeze feels nice too. Sort of like a secret handshake between girls, aged twelve.

He says, "Okay, friend. How about getting the salads out of the fridge while I slice the bread. And open the wine. Do you like wine? I didn't know if I should open a red or white."

Violetta Armour

"I like white if you have it," I say as I open the refrigerator door and laugh. The only thing in it are two salads. "Do you ever eat at home? There's no food in here."

"What? A six-pack of beer on the bottom shelf doesn't count? And there's a hunk of cheddar cheese in there somewhere."

Mike makes a big gesture of pulling out my chair. I make a note to start having Teddy to do that at home. Good date training.

He spoons a good chunk of the pot roast, carrot and potatoes onto my plate, then raises his wine glass and we chink, chink. "To good friends."

The meat is moist and tender. "Mmm. Delicious."

During dinner he tells me about growing up in Chicago in an Italian neighborhood with lots of kids playing on the street until dark in the summer months. How you couldn't get away with anything because somebody's mother was always hanging out of a window checking on the street gang.

"I'm jealous. I always wanted siblings. My parents were older and even our neighborhood was old with few kids my age," I say.

"How about here? Do your neighbors have kids for Cathy and Ruby to play with?"

"No, we're living in the older section of town. Actually, it's the house my husband grew up in. Maybe I told you last time…with his mother, Baba. She has lots of room. It's homey and we're good for her too. She loves to cook and fuss over us."

"Is that hard for you? Being in your husband's home?"

"Hasn't been particularly." I say. "I think it would have been harder to stay at our home in Phoenix without him. I never spent a lot of time at his parents' home. We met in college at I.U. He did take me home a few times, but we moved to Arizona right after we graduated and got married."

Mike reaches across the table and puts one of his hands on mine. "Mary, I mentioned it before but I'll say it again. I'd like to know everything about Stan that you'd like to tell me."

I nod and blink back the tears coming on at his kindness.

He clears the table and when I get up to help, he says to leave the dishes, but I insist that we do them since he has an early shift in the morning. It's comfortable being together in the kitchen.

"And now, the final touch to any good dinner."

He reaches up and pulls down a small white box from the top of the refrigerator. It is tied with a piece of white ribbon, which he unties carefully. Nestled inside are two perfect brownies, each the size of a third-world country.

"You like?" he asks, looking quite pleased with himself.

"I like," I answer and then say, "Do we have to dirty two more plates? We just did the dishes."

"We could eat them out of the box," he says. So we do. I'm not only liking the brownies but him as well.

When it comes time to say good-night, he says, "I should have come and picked you up. Now you have to drive home alone in the dark. I'm going to follow you to make sure you get home okay."

"Don't be silly. It's not that far. I'll be fine."

"Then would you please call me when you get home?"

"If it makes you feel better, I will. And thanks for a lovely evening. I feel like I was transported back to happier days. College days, the seventies, great music."

He smiles. "Is it okay to give a friend a good-night hug?"

"Absolutely," I say. "Friends should hug."

And so we do.

When I get home, I see the picture of Stan and me. I didn't think of him once during the evening until Mike mentioned him. This makes me somewhat relieved, but also sad, like saying good-bye to a friend I've known for a long time.

TEDDY

George asked me if I wanted to come over and watch Sunday football with him. He's an Indianapolis Colts fan but likes baseball more than football. Big Cubbies fan. Today I'm teaching him how to do an Excel spreadsheet, so he can keep track of baseball scores come spring.

"All this fancy technology stuff is something, Teddy. I used to keep track in this little green book." He holds up a small spiral notebook. "Change can be good, but sometimes hard to accept. People like things to stay the same, things they are familiar with. Like today, I saw in the paper that Montgomery Wards is going out of business. Closing all 250 stores. Back in the day, we called it Monkey Wards. Brings back a ton of memories."

I settle in for a good story.

"The house I grew up in was a Monkey Ward house. Delivered to us all the way in western Colorado by railroad from Chicago. It came in sections, and my dad and the other ranchers put it together."

"A house that came from a catalog? Wow, that's strange."

"No, what was strange was that there wasn't a square corner to be found by the time that amateur crew got through. Barn raising is a little different than putting together a two-story house. A bit drafty when the snow blew in from the mountains and at nine-thousand feet elevation, that was quite often.

"But that Monkey Ward catalog was something special. We couldn't wait to get our hands on it. The nearest store, besides the little corner grocery, was thirty-five miles away. We'd sit for hours all winter long and look at all the things we wanted to have. When the new catalog came, we put the old one in the outhouse."

"For reading? You had a light in the outhouse?"

"Not exactly. See, we often didn't have the soft Charmin folks use today. A sheet out of the catalog did the job. The men used all the pages with ladies clothing. They saved the men's pages with tools, so they could do some light reading in the daylight hours while…well, while passing the time I should say."

"Wow, that's hard to imagine. Having to go outside to use the bathroom. Wasn't it cold in the winter?"

"You bet it was. And we had an old goose that used to nip at my sister, so if she went out at night, I had to go with her to chase old Gustav off." He slaps his knee and emits a laugh.

"But getting back to changes, when I came home from the war, I brought my parents a little hibachi grill from Japan that they could cook their beautiful beef steaks on. When you live on a cattle ranch, you're often short of cash, but never beef.

"My mother talked my dad into installing indoor plumbing in the new Monkey Ward house since the floor plan included a real honest-to-gosh bathroom. Only one bathroom upstairs for two adults and five kids, but boy, it sure beat walking to the outhouse when you woke up on a cold morning. Anyway, when I got home with the hibachi, my dad said, 'Son, we've gone to Hell in a hand basket.'"

"Oh?"

"Yep, we used to cook inside and do our business outside. Now we're cooking outside and doing our business inside."

I laugh. I could listen to George's stories all night. This night we polish off the bean soup Baba sent with me.

"I've had so much of this delicious ham 'n bean soup, Teddy, it's a good thing we don't have to run to an outhouse. A fella might not make it in time."

MARY

I'm always looking for ways to make the store better. Ideas come from the craziest places. Like last week at the grocery store. Every Wednesday I take Baba grocery shopping on senior discount day. A whopping ten per cent off all purchases except liquor. A discount, plus free coffee and donuts, is quite the draw and the place is swamped with oldsters shuffling through the aisles with all the time in the world. Some in motorized carts and many with a companion. You cannot be in a hurry. It's a slow study in human nature.

My most recent adventure I call the *Case of the Missing Cart*. Baba likes to push the cart. It's easier for her to hold onto the cart with her arthritic hip, so I usually walk beside her and help her reach things off the higher shelves.

We make the mistake of abandoning the cart in produce. She is off squeezing a melon and I'm checking out the beautiful, deep-purple Japanese eggplants for a new recipe I saw on the Food Channel. Wonder if James ever makes Ratatouille? Rosetta wouldn't because it involves lots of chopping, and she said she sees enough knives in surgery.

When we return to where our cart should have been, it's gone. I tell Baba to hang out in produce—that's her favorite section anyway—while I track down the missing cart.

I walk up and down the aisles and, sure enough, in aisle four, a frail man is pushing Baba's cart. He's examining a bottle of salad dressing, which he has pulled off the shelf. I approach him carefully so I won't startle him or cause him to drop the bottle.

"Excuse me, sir, I believe that's my cart." I recognize the three-pound bag of onions Baba put in it. And the bag of Honey Crisp apples, which cost twice as much as any other apples, but once you've had them, there's no going back.

He glares at me as if he might clobber me with the cane hanging on the side of his cart, then says in a stern voice, "This is not your cart. This is my cart. See those cans of cat food. I put them in myself." Evidently, he added them after he confiscated Baba's cart.

I peer into the cart to see what other items he may have also placed but don't see anything else that belongs to him. He walks away when I notice a box of feminine products in the bottom corner which I bought. I place my hand on his cart gently and point to the box, "And would that box be yours also?"

He glances down and his face turns red. I feel bad for embarrassing him, but I didn't want to begin our shopping all over. He lets go of the cart as if it's a burning bush and says, "Then where is my cart? What have you done with it?"

"I don't have your cart, sir, but let's walk back to produce. That's where you might have found this one."

He frowns, but takes his cane and hobbles beside me as I push the cart. Sure enough, when we get to cabbage and broccoli, there appears to be an abandoned cart. The frown is replaced by a knowing glance. "There it is. That's my cauliflower."

I transfer the cans of cat food and then I ask him, "What's your kitty's name?"

"It's not my kitty. It's my wife's. But she's not here anymore. Up and died and left me with a finicky cat. One who only eats the expensive stuff. See this can?" He holds up a tin with a fancy feline pictured wearing a jeweled collar. "Fifty-nine cents. Turns her nose up at the three-for-a-dollar kind." He shakes his head, and I notice a tear in his eye.

I try to offer some words of comfort. "I bet she's a beautiful cat."

"No, she's mangy. Getting old… like me. I should have gone first."

"You never told me her name."

"Amelia," he says tenderly.

"That's lovely." I'm not sure if that's the wife's name or the cat's, but think it best not to ask.

"She *was* lovely," he says as he puts his cane on the cart handle and pushes away. I'm about to let him go when I gently take his elbow.

Violetta Armour

"I'm sorry about your wife. I know how much it hurts. I lost my husband and he left me far too soon also."

He looks at me and the anger I saw on aisle four is gone, and in its place, a tender expression. "Thank you, Miss. Thank you for your kindness."

Now I'm the one with the tear in my eye as I turn away.

I find Baba scrutinizing the tomatoes, selective of ones that make the grade.

"There you are," she says as she places the tomatoes in our cart. "So you found ours. I saw you talking to that old man," she says as if she's a spring chicken. "Sometimes old people forget where they put things," she informs me.

"Yes, Baba, they do. And sometimes they remember things they wish they could forget."

As we leave the store without further altercations, we pass the courtesy station with the free coffee and donuts. Two little old ladies are sitting on the bench, and it looks like they're sharing a donut. I hear one say, "I love seeing you here each Wednesday, Edna."

"Me, too. I can't wait to tell you about my granddaughter's latest escapade. She's driving my daughter crazy. Granddaughter is as headstrong as her mother was. And I love it."

They giggle like girls on the playground, and a thought occurs to me. How many wonderful stories they must have to share. A lifetime of them. Why not a book club for seniors? Not young seniors. Old seniors. No one under seventy. I bet it would be a hoot. I can't wait to get back to the bookstore to plan how I will get the word out. Free donuts might be a good incentive. Free anything. Seniors love free.

TEDDY

I'm stuffing my face with Baba's tacos at dinner. They're so good you'd think she grew up in Mexico instead of Bulgaria. She had never eaten a taco before I brought some home from Miguel's on Main Street after a ball game. Baba's somewhat suspicious of take out—thinks anything good should come only from her kitchen. After grilling me where I got them, she tasted one and said, "This is good, Teddy, but I can make for you better. Don't give your money to Mr. Miguel. No charge in my kitchen."

She was right. Hers are better. And free. And she always makes tamale corn with them.

While Baba grills me on food, Mom grills me on the what good things happened today.

"I thought we were going to stick to weird stuff," I say.

"Okay then, I'll start. My weird day got weirder, " she says.

I chew, swallow, and ask, "How's that?" Glad to be off the hook.

"On second thought I'd better tell you later." She rolls her eyes toward Cathy and I get the message that it's something she doesn't want a five-year-old to hear.

So it's back in my court. "Well, today in physics we made a bridge out of popsicle sticks, strong enough that we could run a remote car over it without it collapsing."

Cathy's eyes rounded. "You get popsicles in your class?"

Ruby says, "Did your car make it over the bridge?"

I laugh. "My team's bridge collapsed, but our car kept going and flew right into the next team's bridge and destroyed that too. Total demolition of both bridges. We'll start over tomorrow."

After dinner, while Mom and I are cleaning up the kitchen, she whispers to me, "Sheldon Parks fell off the shelf today."

"Who's Sheldon Parks?"

Mom looks at me like I'm supposed to know. "Gertrude's father in biography. In the little blue urn."

"He's read all the biographies? Moving on to mystery?"

"Teddy, not funny." She gives me the disapproving look mothers are so good at.

"Mindy was dusting the shelf and knocked him over. If he had landed on the carpet he might have survived, but the urn hit the edge of the bottom shelf."

"Mom, it's a little late for him to survive."

Another disapproving look.

"Does Mindy know what was in the urn?"

"No, I never told her about him. I meant to, but kept forgetting. And I'm not telling now. She would feel awful."

"Didn't she see the ashes fall out?"

"Yes, they were scattered all over the floor. Then she said, 'Is that potpourri in there? I'll go get the vacuum.'

Of course I had to stop that. Couldn't suck him up like ordinary dust."

"What did you say?"

"I said, 'Don't worry about it, Mindy. The cleaning people are coming tonight. Don't you give it a thought.' I sent her to the children's section to put away the books that had been pulled out all day."

"Are the cleaning people there now?"

"No, that was a little white lie. I got a piece of cardboard and the little hand broom and dustpan and swept them up in a paper cup until I can figure out what to do with them."

"Them? How many people were in the urn?"

"Not them as in people plural, them as in ashes, plural. And what will I say to Gertrude? She comes in once a week and always stops in biography. I hear her talking to him sometime."

'Well, it was an accident. I'm sure she'll understand. Or can you glue the urn back together and put the ashes back?"

"I suppose. Uh…would you help me with that little project?"

"Oh sure, you want an accomplice in your crime. Why not?"

The next day I stop at the store after school, and we patch up the little blue urn with Monkey Glue, and Mom funnels the ashes into it. It's hard to believe this was once a person. A living breathing soul.

It reminds me that it's been a while since I've visited Dad's grave. A lot has changed in our lives, and although some people would say he knows everything that is happening, he might like to hear it from me.

Rosetta

When Luther said he'd like to visit his father's grave and asks if I would go with him, of course, I couldn't refuse. It's a cold day and we bundle up. The cemetery is void of cars and visitors.

As we stand beside Stan's gravestone with the wind whipping dried leaves around our feet, Luther feels the need to justify his visit. "I don't know why I wanted to come here. Just seems like the respectful thing to do"

"That's nice. I wish you could have known him. I blame myself that you didn't."

"Please, Mom, don't say that. What you did was admirable. Going it alone. You said the sixties were a hotbed of racial tensions. Could you tell me some things about him?"

"He loved basketball, so you got that gene for sure," I laugh. "Besides looking like Teddy does now, he was like him in many ways. A sweet boy. Had a lot of friends but never cocky about it. Showed respect for his parents, which I liked. I never saw him with his parents, but it was the way he spoke about them. They were quite traditional, came from the *old country* as he often said. He seemed protective of them in some ways."

"Would it be weird if I asked Mary to tell me some things about him? I don't even know what kind of work he did, what his favorite food was. Did he have any hobbies? I mean you knew him as a teen. I wonder what kind of man he became. It would be nice to know."

"Mary would enjoy that. Why don't you ask her?"

Luther starts to say something when car tires crunch on the gravel. It stops and Teddy gets out. He doesn't appear to see us.

Luther says, "Gosh what are the odds that we would both come here on the same day—a cold day in winter? What do we do now?"

I say, "Just start walking."

TEDDY

I'm surprised to see another car here on a cold winter day and then even more surprised to see Rosetta and Coach Luther heading toward me.

"Hey, Coach. What are you doing here?"

"Hey, Teddy," he says, and then Rosetta adds, "We were just paying our respects to your dad since we were in the cemetery."

"That's nice of you. Do you have family here too?"

"No, but you know my mother is not doing well. The doctors are not giving us much hope at this point, and as much as we hate to think about final arrangements, we thought we would explore some of our options. Whether it would be Middleburg or Chicago."

"I'm sorry," I say.

"Do you come here often?" Coach asks.

"Probably not as often as I should." I pull my hat down over my ears. "I did when we first moved here. Came every Saturday, and crazy as it sounds, talking to Dad helped me get through that first year. I was coming today to...well, to sort of bring him up-to-date on my life. Not that it's all that exciting but—"

Coach says, "You told me he was a superstar on the basketball team. He'll be glad to hear that you're playing varsity this year."

"I am? Awesome. Did you post that already?"

"Ooops...going to do that Monday. So keep it under your hat till then."

"Thanks, Coach. Thanks a lot. I sure didn't expect to get that news here today. Wow, I'm excited."

Coach blows on his hands, then says, "With so many seniors graduating last year, we're going to be a young team, rebuilding, but we've got a strong lineup."

Violetta Armour

Rosetta tugs on his arm. "Luther, we should let Teddy get on to his dad visit before he freezes out here. Save your ball talk for Monday."

"Yes, ma'am," he answers and looks at me like he's been scolded by the boss. "Later, Teddy." He gives me a wink as he passes by.

I approach Dad's stone and touch the corner like I always do. "Hi, Dad. Maybe you heard that conversation. Good news, huh?"

As their car pulls away, I take a seat on the dead grass, my normal posture, my arms around my knees. The ground is cold so I won't last long in this position as I begin my monologue. "I don't know where I left off last time, but here's what's happening in my world. I love working at the bookstore. Did I even ever tell you that Mom owns a bookstore? She and Rosetta—that's Coach Luther's mom—are partners. It's awesome with all the stuff she has going on there. Great place to hang out. She even set up a teen corner with beanbag chairs, and a lot of my friends come in."

I stand up and take small jumps in place to stay warm.

"That's another thing. I have friends. A couple of guys who play ball, but I guess my best friends are still Joe and Mindy, although *they* are no longer best friends. I introduced them last year, and it was like this perfect match. Mindy tutored Joe while he recuperated from his burns and missed so much school. Then Joe goes to a burn camp and falls in love with Tara from Nebraska. Breaks Mindy's heart, so I am trying to console her like she did me last year when I first moved here.

"In fact, she helped me so much I was beginning to have feelings for her more than a friend. Isn't that what happens when patients fall in love with their psychologist? But I figured Joe needed her more than I did, but now….now…who knows? And then the most popular girl in the school, Patti, asked me to the Sadie Hawkins dance, which made me feel good, but most of the time, I kept thinking about Mindy home all alone.

"Most of the time I'm with Mindy I'm laughing cause she's such a goofball. I wish I could ask you how many girls you dated before you married Mom, but if you were alive, I probably wouldn't be talking to you about this at all, would I? I mean kids don't talk about their love lives with their parents. I could talk to George, but he's kinda old. I'm sure dating was different way back then—what did they call it—courting?

"You would love George's stories, Dad, about growing up on the ranch.

When he's working at the cemetery again next spring, I'll have him tell you some of his tales."

It's so cold and I figure that's probably enough of an update for now. Touching the corner of the stone, I say, "Bye, Dad. I miss you." Last year I couldn't say that without crying. This year it's still a tug on my heart but no tears.

I hurry to my car, but when I reach it, I turn around and run back and jingle the car keys. "I thought you might want to know, I drove here myself." And now the tears do come.

MARY

Rosetta pops in to the bookstore after her shift at the hospital.

I act as if she's a new customer. "Hi there. Can I interest you in something you can't put down? Romance? Suspense? Historical fiction?"

She grins at me. "Nice greeting you have there, Mary. Came by to say 'Hi,' but I am ready for a new book. They're predicting snow all weekend, so it's a good time to curl up and read. What do you recommend?"

"What are you in the mood for?"

"I'm finishing another Patricia Cornwell novel with that medical examiner Kay Scarpetta. I like the series, but I get enough of that jargon on the job. I'm ready for something else."

"I have a great suggestion for you, but first let me tell you what I just read about Patricia Cornwell in an author newsletter I subscribe to. Did you know her father walked out on the family on Christmas Day, 1961, and the kids were taken in by Ruth Bell Graham, wife of the preacher Billy Graham? Ruth is the one who first recognized Patricia's literary talents. And even more interesting is that Cornwell is a direct descendent of the abolitionist, Harriet Beecher Stowe."

"You're a wealth of information. Now how about that good book?"

"For a snowy weekend, I can't think of anything better than a book by Rosamund Pilcher. I'm sure you've read *The Shell Seekers*."

"Loved it. Does she have another one?"

"I recommend *Coming Home*."

I turn to the computer, which lists one on the shelf. "Yes. Follow me."

I pull it off and hand it to Rosetta. "I'm envious that you get to spend the weekend with this love story. Britain during WW II, wonderful characters, beautiful settings. You're going to love it—I promise."

"Money-back guarantee?" she asks with a smile.

"Absolutely. It was a movie or a mini-series on TV a few years ago."

"Speaking of movies, James and I are going to a movie tomorrow night. Trying to decide between *Erin Brokovich*, *Castaway* or *Perfect Storm*. Would you like to join us?"

"Thanks, but I might have a perfect night brewing myself."

"Really? Tell me."

"Weather permitting, Mike and I are driving to Indianapolis tomorrow for an Independent Booksellers' workshop and then we'll have dinner in the city."

"Sounds good. So, things are going well?"

"I think so. He's so considerate. Not rushing me into anything. I mean how many lunches and dinners have we had and still never kissed? A kiss on my hand doesn't count, does it?"

"What? Never? Does he need a shot of testosterone or what? And absolutely, a real kiss has to be lips to lips. Are you hoping tomorrow's the night?"

"I wouldn't refuse him."

"Okay, girlfriend, I'm going to curl up with this good book, and you curl up somehow with Mike. I'll be waiting for a full report on Sunday."

After Rosetta leaves, I think about Mike's patience. He's probably afraid I'll bolt if he comes on too strong, too soon. But I enjoy being with him and he's in my thoughts when I'm not. Should I make the first move so he'll know I'm ready. Ready for what? Ready to feel I'm special to someone again.

MARY

During the early evening on Friday, the storm is brewing and continues through the night. A prediction of six to eight inches of snow on Saturday.

Mike calls me early Saturday morning. "We should postpone our trip to Indy," he says. "Roads will be bad, and although I'm off duty, I should stick close to home. I'm sure to get called in with some type of accident on a slick highway. Why not come here for lunch? We can hang out. Rent a movie?"

"Sounds good to me." I picture his empty fridge. "How about I pick up some groceries on my way over? I make a decent omelet and my chocolate chip cookies aren't bad either."

"Deal," he says.

The grocery store is packed with customers stocking up for the storm, but I finally get through the check-out. I swing by the bookstore on the way to Mike's. Mindy and Teddy are working today. "If the storm gets bad, business could be slow and we might have to close early. I'll check in with you in a few hours."

As I pull into Mike's driveway, he's shoveling the walk, but as soon as he sees me, he comes to help. Always the gentleman, he takes the bags and tells me to go on into the house, out of the blowing snow.

In the kitchen, as I'm pulling groceries from the bags, he comes over to me and pulls me close to him. "I'm so glad to see you, Mary," he whispers in my ear and keeps me in his hug. I back away a bit, but he pulls me closer. "I'm glad we're not going anywhere. I just want to be alone with you."

His tone is so serious that I manage to step back and look into his eyes. "Is everything all right?"

He doesn't answer me right away. Just looks at me with the weirdest expression. "Everything is fine." Then he laughs. "That is, if you got plenty of bacon. I'd hate to send you back out in this storm."

"What?" I say in mock surprise.

"The storm is nothing compared to the lines at the store. People are in a full-panic mode. Darn it, I left the cookie sheet in the car. I wasn't sure if your third-world kitchen would have one. I like to do the bacon in the oven on a cookie sheet, and then I'll need it for the cookies."

"I'll get it," he says, "Anything else in the car?"

"Check the front seat just in case."

"Got it," he says, but when I turn around, after searching in the cupboards for a mixing bowl, he's still standing there, looking at me again with a wistful expression.

"What is up with you today?" I ask. I glance down at my clothes. "Did I forget to button my shirt or what?"

"I'm going, I'm going," he says.

I wash my hands and reach for a towel. Next to it sits a notebook, and scrawled on it is *Kimberly. Sunday 8 p.m.* His wife's name is Kimberly. I hope they resolve their custody issue.

When Mike returns, I broil the bacon and whip up the omelets. We clean up the kitchen and I set aside the ingredients I'll need later for the chocolate chip cookies. The snow is falling steadily, and I call the bookstore to check on things, but it goes to voice mail. I leave a message.

Teddy calls me back in a few minutes. "Sorry I couldn't get to the phone Mom. I know you don't like it to go to voice mail at the store, but it's been busy. Guess people want to curl up with a good book in a storm."

"Do you need me to come in?" I ask.

"No, we're doing fine."

I hang up, but think I should check back in thirty minutes or so.

"More coffee?" Mike asks.

"Please. Did you say you had some movies on VCR? I hope they're not all police chase scenes."

"Of course not. I have a great selection." He goes to the cabinet under the TV and pulls out a handful of Disney movies. Which princess do you prefer? *Cinderella* or *Beauty and the Beast.*"

I laugh. "Nothing wrong with *happily ever after* on a snowy day."

I settle in on the sofa and wrap my arms around my knees. "No wonder so many marriages don't work. Little girls' early conditioning on marriage expectations is pretty unrealistic, thanks to Disney. I love the guy, but…"

"Was your marriage good?" he asks.

"Better than most. We did have our share of differences, but we worked through them. Of course, now I just remember the good parts."

He comes and sits beside me and runs a finger through my hair. "Mary, Mary, Mary," he says. "I like your hair." He strokes my cheek. "And your cheek. And I like your pretty blue eyes." He cups my chin in his hands, "I've come to like so much about you."

His lips are so close to mine that I'm sure he's going to kiss me. Finally.

But instead his next words are quite the opposite. "And that's why this is going to be so hard to say, but …" He shakes his head, closes his eyes, and I get a sinking feeling in my tummy. "Kimberly called last night. She wants to give our marriage another try. Says she's come to her senses and we belong together, and we need to make a real home for Jessica."

I can't breathe. I feel like something is gripping my chest. I say, "Of course you need to think of Jessica. She's only…."

He interrupts, "I don't know what to do. I have no feelings for Kimberly. Well, I have feelings, but they aren't good ones. I can't imagine living with her again, but when I consider Jessica, I wonder, should I try?"

"I don't know what to tell you. That's a decision you need to make." The queasy feeling in my stomach intensifies. A twinge of anger joins it.

"If I hadn't met you, I might consider it, but, as crazy as it might sound…you and I. I mean we haven't even kissed yet, but believe me, I've wanted to. I've only held back to give you time, time to be sure you're ready. I don't know how you feel, but I don't want to give you up. If there's such a thing as second chances, you might be my second chance."

"But Jessica. She's five years old. She needs a father in her life," I manage.

"Could you answer me this for now. Do you have feelings for me?"

I'm not sure how honest to be at this point. I say, "Of course I do. I wouldn't be here if I didn't. I like you a lot. But I don't want to stand in the way of a family being together. It's something you need to think about seriously. And it might be easier if I weren't in the picture while you do that." I climb to my feet and head toward the door for my coat.

"Mary, please wait. Don't go. Please. You already are in the picture.

What we have is so nice. I shouldn't have said anything today. Now I've ruined it. I wanted to be open and honest with you."

"And I appreciate that. I really do." I glance at the kitchen and say, "If you don't mind, we'll pass on the cookies. I need to leave now. I'm going to check on the kids at the store."

He's right beside me as I put on my coat. He takes me in his arms and holds me closely. I don't resist. To think I could have found happiness again. What did I tell myself about men with baggage earlier? I feel like he just asked me to carry the entire three-piece set of matched luggage. No, more like dragging a steamer trunk.

As much as I hate myself for doing it, I burrow my head into his shoulder. He keeps holding me and whispering, "I'm such a fool. After all you've been through. Please don't go."

He tilts my head and gently wipes a tear off my cheek. Then softly, he kisses my cheek, my forehead, my neck, and then his lips find mine. Our first kiss is not how I imagined it would be, yet it is still so sweet. And a bit salty too from my tears.

Time to leave. Past time to leave.

Mary

I leave Mike's house and drive to my safe haven—the bookstore. The roads are slippery and I creep along, but it gives me time to think. What a foolish notion I had—to think that I might find a meaningful relationship again. People talk about second chances. Not for me. I don't have the energy now to deal with someone else's problems. I have everything I need in my life right now. A business I care about, three children I love, and friends. Well, one friend, Rosetta. I haven't had time to develop others, but I do care about my customers.

When I reach the store, it's deserted of customers. Teddy's voice chatters from the children's section. He and Mindy are sitting on the floor and they don't notice me. Their friendship makes me smile. Teddy sits with his long legs stretched out and Mindy is sitting between them, her back to him as he holds out an oversized picture book in front of her, *The Little Engine That Could*, and reads, "I think I can. I think I can."

He closes the book and says, "I loved this one. Okay, your turn to pick out your favorite."

When Mindy gets up, she notices me. "Hi, Mrs. K. You're back."

"Hey, Mom," says Teddy. "I thought you were going to give yourself a day off."

"A slight change of plans. Things look pretty quiet here. I doubt we'll have much business. The roads are deserted. We should close shop."

"Whatever you say, boss," Teddy says. "It was busy this morning, but no one has been in for a while. As you can see, we are reverting to our childhood here."

"Teddy, make sure Mindy gets home safely, and then you head home too. I'll close up and be there shortly."

They look at each other and Teddy says, "We were sort of planning on spending the day together. Can Mindy stay at our house till the storm passes?"

Mindy chimes in. "Yeah, as long as we're reading children's books, we might as well have a play date too."

"Of course it's okay. Be sure to let your parents know where you are."

"I will," Mindy says.

"And, Teddy, drive carefully. The roads are getting slippery."

"Will do," he answers.

"And call me when you get home."

Teddy turns toward me. "Mom, are you okay? You seem a little...well, nervous. Do you want us to stay here with you? Or better yet, we should all leave." He looks out the window. "It's coming down pretty fast now."

"I'll be right behind you after I run today's receipts."

I should leave too, but right now the bookstore is a refuge to me. It provides a place to be alone to nurse my disappointment. I pour a cup of coffee and sit in my favorite reading chair. Enya is playing softly in the background. Footnote curls around my legs and settles in the opposite wing chair, eyes me for a minute, then Enya lulls him to seep. I'd better check his food supply before leaving.

The snow is coming down harder now, and I should close shop and head home myself, but the books are comforting to me in a way I don't exactly understand. Perhaps because books have only given me pleasure in my life, rarely heartaches and disappointments. Other than the few that made me wonder how they were ever published.

One customer told me about a formula to use when deciding if you should continue on with a book you're not sure about. Subtract your age from one hundred, and that's the number of pages you should read before you decide to quit...or throw it against the wall.

My silent retreat is broken when my cell phone rings from my sweater pocket. I take it out and see Mike's name. No way I can talk to him now, so I let it go to voice mail. But it startles me from my peaceful moment, so I walk through the store re-shelving books and turning out lights. I lower the thermostat a notch. No use heating the whole place for one kitty who has a splendid fur coat.

When I reach the front of the store, I stare out the front windows. Main Street is deserted. I'd better print out a closed sign for the door, although I doubt anyone will come by to see it. If schools can have snow days, so can bookstores.

I'm running the daily receipts when the front door opens with a blast of cold air. I turn and see Mike. He rushes behind the counter and extends his arms like he's going to give me a big bear hug, then thinks better of it. Instead, he takes both my hands in his—still in gloves. "Mary, I was so worried. I shouldn't have let you go out alone in this storm and you weren't answering your phone. I had to know you're okay."

I start to speak, but he keeps talking.

"I was such a jerk to ruin our day. I am so sorry."

"Please, don't be sorry. You were being honest, and it's better for me to know now before—" I stop because I don't want to say *before I am in too deep*.

"Before what, Mary?"

I plunge ahead, risking better judgement. "Before my feelings for you became stronger. It would hurt more then."

"Then you do have feelings for me?"

"Of course I do. I mean, I like you a lot, but until you decide what your relationship will be with Kimberly, I...I need to stay out of it."

"That's fair enough. Honestly, I can't see myself with her again. Once that trust is gone…"

"But there's Jessica." I say.

"Yes, there is Jessica." He takes his hat off and rubs his hair.

"Kimberly's coming over tomorrow, and I'll see what has brought this change of heart for her. I am doubtful and suspicious that it's in Jessica's best interests…or that Kimberly cares about me at all."

"Yes, but she certainly deserves to be heard."

"Can I call you after we meet?"

I hesitate. "I want to be your friend, but…but it's best if we don't talk right now. As long as you are still married, I want to step out of the picture. Sorry, but that's how I feel right now. Hope you can understand that."

He looks dejected, but nods. "I do, and I'll respect your decision. But one more request I hope you'll allow."

"What's that?" I ask, my heart beginning to race.

"If you're closing the store, can I follow you home? I want to be sure you're safe."

I smile. "I guess I could allow that. I'll be about five minutes." I motion to the coffee station. "There's one cup left in that pot if you'd like some. And please check that I've turned it off. Don't want my dream business going up in flames."

One dream shattered today is enough.

TEDDY

Middleburg is running their annual blood drive, and a lot of the football and basketball players are donating. They made a big pitch for it the night of the Father-Son Banquet. Some of the guys say, "Yeah, free cookies and juice after...I'm in."

The drive has grown into such a big deal that some of the parents are hosting a cookout at Patriot Park for those who donate. They're serving foods high in iron. Spinach salads, beans, and red meats. Someone said they are slipping in some ground liver disguised as a burger—yuk.

Mindy is bummed because she wants to donate but can't. You have to weigh at least 110 pounds, and she tips the scales at only 105 after a meal. She compensates her disappointment by making big charts with the ten reasons why donating blood is good for you. Mindy convinced a lot of the girls to sign up when she told them a single blood donation of one pint burns about 650 calories. She tells them, "That's more than you would burn in a thirty-minute run."

Kids are comparing their blood types, and a lot of teasing is going on from the A+ types who say that is proof that they must be smarter than anyone else. O positive is the most needed type, often called the universal donor because it can be used with many other blood types.

The hardest match to find is O negative because they can only receive a transfusion from an 0 negative donor. That is what the lab technician tells me when he discovers I'm an O negative. He says, "You might want to consider donating several times a year because your blood type is so rare."

"So do I get extra cookies today?" I ask.

He says, "It's quite unusual that we have two O negatives today. That doesn't happen often."

"Who's the other one?" I ask out of curiosity.

"Well, I'm not at liberty to say," he says and then he looks around the group. His eyes fall on Luther. He smiles at me and says, "You might, however, check with your coach."

TEDDY

The next time I'm at George's, he shows me some photos in an old scrapbook, the kind with little black corners holding the pictures in place like Baba has in her scrapbooks. George is probably older than Baba, but they're alike in many ways. I should invite him over for a real dinner instead of bringing leftovers. I think he had a good time at our New Year's Eve party last year and Baba is always happy to set another place at the table.

He is showing me what he calls a brand book, and he turns to the page that shows his parents' ranch cattle brand. It's an A/W. "Dad always said we had a starve-to-death cow operation."

I say, "I'm confused. Who's starving? The cows or your family?"

George laughs. "I think he joked that we didn't make a lot of money in the cattle business. But I never remember going hungry. We always had lots of beef and Mom had a summer vegetable garden that fed us all winter."

George takes a sip of his coffee and looks kinda sad. "Then one year the Bureau of Land Management sent their representative out to the house. He came wearing his stuffy suit and necktie, which set Dad off right away.

"Dad said, 'Wouldn't you think a guy calling on country folk would at least wear some decent ranch clothes like a pair of Levi's?' My dad always said suits were just for marryin' and buryin'.

"When the BLM guy told Dad they were going to have to cut his cattle permits in half, he couldn't understand why Dad was so angry. I still remember what Dad said to him as I hid on the stairway out of sight, but close enough to hear what was going on in the kitchen.

"The guy said something like, 'No reason to be so upset, is there? You can still keep half your cattle.' He didn't get it. Then Dad said to the pompous guy who didn't have the decency to be sorry for what he had to do, 'Tell me this, pardner, how would you like it if next year your salary was cut in half? And then your boss said, 'But don't worry, you can keep the other half.'

The guy slunk out the door.

"Mom had been sitting there at the kitchen quietly and when the bastard—pardon my French—left, she got up and walked behind Dad's chair. She put her arms around his neck and said, 'We'll be fine, Stuart. We'll make it just fine.' They were rugged people, Teddy. Tough when they had be, yet kind as all get out. Then Mom said, 'And to think I gave him the last piece of my good banana bread. Should have sprinkled it with black pepper instead of powdered sugar.'

"I'll never forget what Dad said. 'Some people are so crooked they can hardly lay in bed at night.' Then he pulled Mom onto his lap and held her. I snuck back up the stairs thinking this was a private moment."

Driving home, I wish I could have seen Mom and Dad grow old together. It was no wonder the church sign the other day said, *Grow Old With Me, the Best is Yet to Be.*

ROSETTA

When Dad calls to tell me Mom has passed peacefully in her sleep, I dress as quickly as I can. I toss off my pajamas and throw them, my toothbrush and a change of clothes into my gym bag in case he wants me to spend the night. With trembling fingers, I call James who's on a business trip. I didn't cry when Dad told me, but as soon as I try to tell James, the tears pour out. "James, Mom has passed. She's gone."

"I'm so sorry. I'll call the airlines and get the next flight home."

"Let's wait until I talk to Dad. He might want me to stay with him."

"I'll wait to hear from you. I can hold a seat for twenty-four hours, so I'll look into what's available. I love you, Rosetta."

I have driven to my parents so many times on the two-lane back roads that I could find my way blindfolded. It feels that way this morning because the tears blur my vision.

When I arrive Dad is waiting for the coroner and the mobile transport. We hug and cry, consoling each other as best we can. He leads me to the bedroom where Mom is laying partially covered with her favorite flowered quilt that Grandma made, soft to the touch from so many washings. She looks so peaceful, so rested, so beautiful.

"Do you want some time alone with her, Rosetta?" Dad asks.

"No, Dad, stay with me please. There's nothing I can say to Mom that I wouldn't want you to hear. I hardly ever think of one of you without the other, and I've been so lucky to have you both as parents."

"I was the lucky one. Fifty-two years of marriage and three years before that." He stuffs his hands in his pockets, shakes his lowered head, and rocks back and forth on his heels. "But I wanted more. We talked a lot about how some day, we'd sit in our rocking chairs on the porch reminiscing."

"Of courses you did. Of course." He sits down in a chair, which has been pulled up close beside her bed. I walk to the back of his chair, put my arms around his neck and nuzzle my head on his shoulder.

"Do you know what time?"

"Not exactly. When I awoke this morning and looked at her—the first thing I always do—I knew she had passed. She usually has a slight little snore, which I came to love and I didn't hear it. I checked her pulse and there was none. That was about five. Then I lay beside her with my arms around her until I called you at seven."

"Wouldn't we all wish to pass so peacefully with our loved one beside us?" I say. In the background music plays softly. "What's the music, Dad?"

"Oh, some of your mother's favorites. Billie Holiday and Nat King Cole. We had them on almost all day yesterday. Did some reminiscing. Even a little dancing. Well, mainly holding your mother up against me. A slight swaying to the music."

"That was a nice way to spend your day together. Alone yet together." I say.

"Actually, Mindy stopped by. I forgot we had set up a tutoring schedule. But she didn't stay. Mom lay down for a while and Mindy and I talked a bit about music in my day—turntables and vinyl's. I was playing a Lena Horne, and when I turned it over, Mindy was surprised to see you could play the other side too."

We both laugh about that, and it feels good for just a minute.

Dad goes on. "Mindy, of course, didn't know most of the old artists, but she's such a curious little thing. She liked the cover of the Lena Horne album and looked up her name on my computer.

"She says to me, 'Here, let me show you. You'll like this, Dr. Stone. There's this new thing called Google. You just go to the Internet and type in what you are looking for and it finds it for you. I think it's called a search engine or something like that."

Mindy was surprised at all the awards Lena won, starting back from the fifties through the eighties. I told her some of the history I remembered. How Miss Horne was one of the first black singers at a white nightclub in New York—the Cotton Club. She could perform there but she couldn't go in the front door. Had to use the back entrance."

I shake my head to express my disbelief.

Dad says, "Mindy was a nice little diversion for me, but we put our tutoring session off for another day."

"What can I do for you now, Dad? Can I make some calls to Chicago?" I try to put on my efficiency hat. I often deal with death daily at the hospital, but here I feel it so differently.

"That would be good. Let me get the address book out for you."

Dad goes to his desk. He shuffles a few things around in his top desk drawer. A man so organized, he now looks confused and lost. I go to help him look. Lying on top of his desk is a crème-colored envelope that says *Rosetta*. "Is this for me?"

"Oh, yes, can't believe I forgot about that. Your mother wrote it not long after you told her about Luther's dad. Your high-school friend."

"You mean Stan?"

"Yes, Stan, Forgive me, Rosetta, my mind is distracted now. I was to give you this from your mother." He hands me the letter.

I don't know what I'm supposed to do with it. "Should I open it now?" I ask.

"That's up to you, honey. Up to you." He hands me the battered address book and walks into the bedroom. I'm left standing there with a letter from my dead mother, possibly talking about Luther's dead father.

I take a deep breath and sit in Dad's wing-back chair. I'm about to open it when the coroner arrives. I stuff it in my purse and answer the door.

MARY

"Mrs. K., what's wrong? You look like you've seen a ghost," Mindy says when I return to the bookstore from doing errands.

"Worse," I answer as I walk to the drinking fountain, take a drink and plop myself in the chair in the self-help section.

"Worse?"

"There's a sign…a huge sign. No, a billboard. It takes up the whole corner."

"What corner? What sign?"

"At 10th and Washington. Where that new strip mall is going in. It's a huge sign about a new bookstore coming soon. Huge sign means huge store and that means it's going to swallow us up. Oh, Mindy, why is this happening now? Just when things are going so well."

I glance up at Mindy who looks perplexed and obviously she has no clue what I'm talking about. "Harms and Global. They're coming. In three months. Our little store will be history. And we have two years left on this lease."

"OMG. It's just like *You've Got Mail*. You saw that movie, didn't you?"

"Yes, I thought it was charming. But I wasn't a bookseller then…nor a widow. Right now love stories make me sad instead of happy."

"Well, I can relate to that for sure." Mindy says, then quickly adds, "I'm sorry, Mrs. K. I didn't mean to imply that Joe breaking up with me is anything as sad as your loss. I'm such an idiot."

"You are not an idiot. Teddy told me what happened and I'm so sorry. It hurts to lose someone you love. Even if they are still alive. Maybe even more because you can see them with someone else."

"Oh, that probably won't happen. She lives in Nebraska." Mindy looks forlorn, but then perks up. "Did you know that *You've Got Mail* was a

Violetta Armour

remake of a 1940 movie starring Jimmy Stewart and Margaret Sullivan? It was called *The Shop Around the Corner*."

"No, I didn't…."

"And in real life the Barnes and Noble on Broadway and 83rd Street in New York did put a little store around the corner out of business. It was called Shakespeare and Company."

"See, that's exactly what I mean. Who can compete with those big boys?"

"Oh, I'm an idiot again. Twice in under three minutes. You didn't need to hear that, did you?"

"I might as well face reality," I say, getting up and walking to the phone. "I need to call Rosetta and James."

"Uh, Mrs. K., it's not my business, but wouldn't it would be better if you talked about this in person with them. I've watched you—all three of you—so many times brainstorming new ideas for the store. It's like you bounce ideas off each other and good things happen."

"Mindy, you are absolutely right, my little brain child. I'll drop by tonight after work and we can talk about this altogether." *Or cry together.*

Mindy says, "Guess I'll go now since you're here. You are here, aren't you?"

"Yes, I am here." I square my shoulders, "And if I have my say about it, I'm going to stay right here."

"That's the spirit, Mrs. K. By the way, Meg Ryan, in real life, got her first computer while she was filming *You've Got Mail*. Cool, huh?"

"How do you know all this stuff?"

"I don't know. Probably when I was cramming for *Teen Jeopardy*."

I'd better start cramming on how to keep a small business running, I tell myself as Mindy heads out the door.

Then she returns. "You know, Mrs. K. You called those big stores super stores. This may not be a super store in size, but it's a super store in every other way. Get it?"

I smile at Mindy's attempt to make me feel better. "I get it. Now we need to convince other shoppers that we are super too."

I plop down in the soft easy chair in the biography section, and Footnote jumps on my lap. He purrs as I stroke him, and it does have a calming effect on me. Mozart's *Marriage of Figaro* is playing softly and adds more comfort. I want to stay positive but still wonder *why now?* When it's going so well. Promotions? We have 'em. And they're working. And the bottom line is improving.

How many book discussion groups? The singles, seniors, mystery, regular children's bedtime stories, daytime story time for preschoolers. *American Girl* parties on Saturdays. The quarterly newsletter. Hosting the book fair at the grade school. Special events each month. James or Baba doing a cooking demo with all the cookbooks on sale. Wearing green on St. Patrick's day and any book with green on the cover is 30% off.

Now I am green with envy at the thought of the thousands of books a large store can shelve in their inventory.

TEDDY

I tell Mindy, "I'm worried about my mom. Ever since she saw that huge billboard about that big box store that's coming soon a mile away, she's not herself. One day she's worried, the next day she says things like, "I'm not going to let them put me out of business."

"Yeah, the other night at closing, I found her in the children's section staring at the mural on the wall. The one with the little boy in bed dreaming of all his favorite bedtime stories. Tears were running down her face. She said something like, 'Oh, Mindy, I wish we could scrape this off the wall and take it with us.'"

"I asked her, 'Where are we going?'"

"Nowhere, I'm afraid. But I have to be realistic. How can we compete or survive with the mega store?"

"So, I quick got her some tissues we always keep on the children's shelf next to *I'll Love You Forever*."

"Why are tissues always there?" I ask.

"Duh, you need to get to know the inventory. I dare you to read that book without crying. We always recommend it as a gift for baby showers."

"See, that's what I'm talking about. Do you think Harms and Global is going to put a box of Kleenex out for their customers? Mom is so sensitive to people's needs."

Mindy nods in agreement. "And I've heard her call a customer when she's unpacking a new book shipment saying, 'Hey, I got a new book in that made me think of you. The jacket cover sounds like everything you love in a book—mystery, romance, English-village setting. Should I set it aside for you?' Who does that in those big stores?"

I shrug in agreement, as if to say, "No one?"

Mindy continues, "They're too big to have that personal touch. I mean your mom is here like 24/7. She knows almost everyone who comes in."

"We have to think of a way to let Mom know how important this store is to Middleburg."

"Maybe *we* don't have to let her know. Maybe, just maybe, her customers need to tell her."

"That's it. You're a genius."

"Why state the obvious?" She laughs and I get that fluttery feeling inside whenever I make her laugh. She may know how smart she is, but she has no idea how cute she is.

ROSETTA

Mary calls and says she wants to spend time with me alone. To console me about my mother's passing. I gladly accept her invitation to come over.

"I'll bring some wine, " she says.

"I'll furnish the cheese."

"And we can whine as long as we need to. You about your loss and me about my bookstore, although I'm not in any way saying my loss is as great as yours," Mary says.

"It would be good for both of us to talk about it—whatever's making our hearts ache right now."

Once we're settled in, Mary says, "The days after the service can be the hardest. After the many casseroles have been eaten, the glassware washed and put away, and your mailbox is no longer full of sympathy cards. That's when it hits—the person is truly gone." She pauses, then continues, "When Stan passed, I was numb with grief. No feelings for anything, except the kids, and those feelings were mingled with so much sadness."

I say, "That's a good description. I feel numb. How long did yours last?"

"I don't remember when it started to wear off, but I almost wish I was numb again. Now I've started to care about things and people and …. and I feel vulnerable again. If you don't care, the loss can't hurt you. I love my bookstore and I don't want to lose it. And although I can't say I loved Mike yet, I was beginning to love being with him."

I glance at Mary. "What are you talking about? You're not with him anymore?"

"I'll explain later." She shrugs it off. "I came here to talk about your loss. So talk to me about your mom. Anything. One of my grief seminars told me that people love to talk about the person they lost. They want to say their name over and over in some way. Sadly, most friends, although they mean well, avoid the subject."

"Something I haven't told you yet. My mom left a letter with my dad. She wrote it shortly before she passed, and I'm not sure if I was supposed to get it the day she wrote it or after. But it did make me feel better."

"In what way?" I ask.

"The night I told her about Stan….you know, after the little dinner party we had, I felt that I had made a huge mistake. She went to bed and didn't even acknowledge it." I wipe away a tear that has dribbled down my cheek. "I was so foolish to burden her with that information when she was so weak."

We take a sip of wine and I continue. "But in her letter she said she was happy that things had come full circle, that I could meet Stan's family. That Luther could know his dad. Not *know* him, but know *of* him. She said she never faulted me for loving him. Although at the time I told her I was pregnant, I didn't think she was understanding. My father did, but she was angry. She always wanted me to have a good education.

"And then…" my voice turns to a whisper although we are the only two in the room. "She said I was probably not the first in our family to love a white boy."

Mary's eyes widen by my choice of words. I smile. "I say *boy* because we were so young. Remember that song—*They tried to tell us we're too young. Too young to really be in love.* Any teenager can relate to that one, huh?"

Mary smiles now too. She says, "I love our girl talk. You're the sister I always wanted but never had. So what did she mean by that part—*not the first one*"?

"She simply alluded to how fair my complexion was. She and Dad are both darker than me. That there must have been a mixed-race relation somewhere in our lineage."

Then I smile. "Stan and I joked once about how his skin was darker than mine in the summer."

Mary looks sad, and I wonder if I should have shared that memory. She senses my apprehension and offers a weak smile. "Yes, he was tan most of the year living in Arizona. I burned after a few hours in the sun. Teddy got his Bulgarian genes and the girls got mine. They'll be slathering that sunscreen on like it's a second skin."

We are quiet for a moment, lost in our memories of Stan. Then she asks, "Have you traced your family tree?"

"No, and I probably won't. Luther might have an interest in doing so but I don't."

Mary says, "Yeah, I've heard horror stories of people who were adopted searching out their birth parents, and sometimes they end up wishing they hadn't. I do have one great story, however, from a customer that I'll share with you another time."

Mary sits up straighter as if she is going to give a full report. "For now I want to say it's not been that long that your mother is gone, but you and your dad might be experiencing what I did when Stan passed. That stunning awareness that people are going on with their lives, and you wonder how and why they can do that when you are still struggling with such a loss. When there is that one person no longer here on earth. And people around you return to their daily routines and you are left alone with your grief, wondering how they can continue to function as though nothing has happened. How and why does the world go on?"

"Exactly what I was thinking the other day. Watching people laughing, and Main Street put up Christmas decorations. I mean I don't expect them to hang black banners, but still it hurts that they act like everything is okay—when clearly it's not and never going to be the same."

"I got a new book in the other day." Mary digs into her purse. "It's small but carries a big message. I'd like you to have it." She pulls out a book with a yellow cover. "It's Max Lucado's *Traveling Light*. Here's one passage that might help. I wish I had it when I was in the first raw stages of grief over Stan." She opens it to the bookmarked page and reads it to me.

"*...the black bag of sorrow is hard to bear. It's hard to bear because not everyone understands your grief. They did at first. They did at the funeral. They did at the graveside. But they don't now...they don't understand. Grief lingers.*

As silently as a cloud slides between you and the afternoon sun, memories drift between you and joy, leaving you in a chilly shadow. No warning, no notice. Just a whiff of the cologne she wore or a verse of a song he loved and you are saying good-bye all over again.

Why won't the sorrow leave you alone?

Because you buried more than a person. You buried some of yourself.

It's as if the human race resides on a huge trampoline. The movements of one can be felt by all. And the closer the relationship, the more profound the exit. When someone you love dies, it affects you.

Her voice breaks as she reads the last line, and we cling tightly to each other.

TEDDY

As Mindy and I brainstorm on how our scheme might work, we decide to include Rosetta and James. After all, it's their store too, but mostly we need to know if they consider our idea totally whacky. We include Mike because of fire regulations. Have extra fire extinguishers on hand. Or the entire Station 43 on stand-by.

Mindy agrees. "It would be pretty awful if while we're trying to save the store, we burn it down instead."

"She does love her candles. It's like a religious ceremony for her the way she's always lighting them at home."

"Religious wouldn't hurt. We sure could use a little help from the man upstairs on this project. Hey, you know those little paper things they put under the candles on Christmas Eve church service when we sing "Silent Night"? We should get some of those. 'Cause if there's wax dripping all over the store, you know who's going to clean it up, don't you?"

"Some lowly hourly employee? One with red hair, by chance?"

"Uh, huh. That would be me. So, do you want to take on that little assignment? Talk to someone at that church you always pass on the way to school? The one whose billboard you like to read?"

"Hey, how do you know about that?" *Did I ever talk to Mindy about my need for inspirational quotes to get me through my first year here?*

"You told me once that sometimes you pass it on purpose just to see what it says. That you miss your Book of Life."

"I did?"

I must have looked surprised because she says, "It's okay. There's nothing wrong with that. I like it that you read church billboards."

"You do?"

"Would you please stop answering everything I say with a question? And will you please look into the candle holders?"

"Okay, Bossy Pants" I say as I salute her. "For someone so small, you sure command a lot of authority."

"Why, thank you. I like being compared to Helena."

"Helena who?" I ask.

"Helena in Shakespeare's *A Midsummer Night Dream.* It's a famous quote. *Though she be but little she is fierce.*"

Yes, fierce pretty much says it. I say, "Our biggest challenge is how do we get the word out to customers who would be willing to participate? Who might want to be part of a 'save the store' project?"

Nothing stumps Mindy. "I can get into the customer database and send emails. I may not reach all the customers, but enough to make it work. And have them help us spread the word….and mum's the word, of course, so *your mum* doesn't have an inkling of what we are planning."

Rosetta and James go along with our scheme. We not only get their approval but their praise and enthusiasm as well. Now all that's left is to get Mike onboard.

TEDDY

I swing into Firehouse 43, which is not far from the bookstore, to see if Mike is working. It would be easier to explain this scheme in person. Luckily, he's on his shift and not out on a call. Sitting at the kitchen table with a couple of the guys. One is reading and the other one has a laptop computer open.

Mike glances up. "Teddy, this is a nice surprise. What brings you here? Are you okay?"

"Well, yes and no." I approach him so I don't have to speak loudly in front of the other guys. "I'm okay, but I'm a little worried about Mom."

Mike's brow furrows, and he gets up. "Let's talk over here." He leads me to a corner of the kitchen away from the table.

"Do you drink coffee? Want a cup?"

I don't normally, but feel grown-up that he asked me, so I say, "Yeah, that would be good." Like we're going to have a real man-to-man talk.

"How do you take it?"

"Uh, I guess however you do," I say.

Mike laughs. "You're not a coffee drinker yet, are you? Let me doctor this up a bit and see how you like it." He pours a cup and adds sugar, then he takes some milk out of the fridge.

I'm thinking I'd rather have milk and cookies, but that's childish. Next thing he might be offering me a beer, but surely not while he's on duty.

He brings two cups to us and we stand there in the corner leaning on the counter. "So, tell me what's going on with your mom. You probably know I care a lot about her."

"I thought so and—"

"And are you okay with that?" He frowns. "She said she hadn't dated anyone since your dad…." His voice trails off.

"Oh, this isn't about that," I reassure him. "It's great that she is seeing you." I take a sip of the coffee, and it tastes bitter.

I must have made a face 'cause Mike says, "That coffee's probably been sitting here all day. Sorry about that."

I wave him off. "It's about the new big bookstore coming to town. You've probably seen the billboards advertising it."

"Yes, I have, but that's months out…according to their sign anyway. Something about next year?"

"She's already worrying about it though. Mindy and I came up with a plan, or scheme—whatever you want to call it—that might show her how important her little store is and how her customers will remain loyal. I hope they will anyway." I take another sip and it doesn't taste as bad as the first one. I heard once that coffee is an acquired taste. "I can't guarantee they will, but we ought to give them a shot at telling her that."

I explain what Mindy and I are planning and ask him two favors. Would he take Mom to dinner that night at the Mexican or Chinese restaurant in the same strip mall, and two, would he approve of the candles we want to use? Perhaps provide extra fire extinguishers?

Mike sets his coffee cup down and runs his hands through his hair while peering down at the floor for a moment. When he looks up, he says, "I'd love to take your mom to dinner. Trust me, I would love to. See, the problem is she's decided we have to cool our heels a bit—"

I interrupt him. "What does that mean? Cool heels? Why?"

Mike sighs. "You deserve honesty. I'm still in the process of getting my divorce, and although I have every intention of going through with it, your mom thinks she shouldn't see me until I do." He shakes his head as if he's not in agreement with her decision. "Make sense?"

I don't know what to say. "I guess so, but gee, how long will that be?"

"We have a court date next month. Not far off, but for someone who wants to be with your mom, it's too far off."

We both are quiet to ponder this. Then I say, "Do you think you could ask her this one night—assuming we can pull this off with the customers—still working on that. Could you ask her for maybe one casual dinner, say to talk about how things are progressing with the court date or something like that?"

"I'd sure be willing to try. Not only for you, but I'd love to have an

Violetta Armour

excuse to see her again other than as a customer. I've been avoiding the bookstore, too, to honor her wishes."

I like this guy and secretly hope he and Mom can work things out.

"Okay, I'll let you know what date we have in mind, and you be working on your dinner date speech."

Mike laughs and puts out his hand out to shake mine. "Deal, Teddy."

I walk away and then turn around. "If this doesn't work out or you don't think it's the right thing to do, we have a back-up plan. I can have Rosetta or James bring her in. I assumed she would be doing something with you."

"I wish."

"And thanks for the coffee. Next thing you know, I'll be hanging out at that new Starbucks. Which I've heard is not cheap."

"If your mom agrees to go out with me soon, I'll buy you a Starbucks gift card."

On the way home, I drive past the Baptist church, and the little billboard has a special message for me. *A candle loses nothing by lighting another candle.*

I think of candles, of customers, of lighting up Mom's life, and I want so much for this to work. Even more so now that I think she could lose her store and Mike both. Doesn't seem fair.

MARY

Back at home, I realize Rosetta and I never did talk about Mike, but that was probably a good thing. I was there for Rosetta, not for myself.

As if she can read my thoughts, my phone rings. "Hey, girlfriend, you didn't tell me what's going on with Mike."

I fill her in as best I can. "Do you think I did the right thing—not seeing him till he works this out with his…" I stop and then go on. "I was about to say ex-wife, and that's the problem. She isn't his ex-wife. What would you do, Rosetta?"

"What does your heart say?"

"It says, 'Keep seeing him.' But my head says no."

"We talked today about not having regrets. That's why I told my mom even against my better judgement about Stan. I didn't want regrets after she was gone. Nobody on their deathbed wishes they were smarter or that they had worked more. I bet they wish they had loved more."

Another call comes in, and Mike's name flashes across my screen. "Rosetta, I gotta go. Call you later."

MARY

"Hello" I say rather breathlessly.

He sounds short of breath too. "You asked that we not see each other, but Mary, I miss you. Can we at least talk?"

I remember Rosetta's words. I don't want regrets, so what if I get hurt again? I take the risk and plunge into the deep end. "I think it would be nice if we talked."

"You do?" He sounds surprised.

I laugh. "Yes, I do, and I miss you too. How are you?"

The relief in his voice is evident. "I'm fine now. Better. Much better. I'm so glad I called. I didn't want to violate any rules and not have you trust me—ever."

"I want to trust you too."

"Can I tell you about my meeting with Kimberly?"

"Yes, I would like that."

"She sounded sincere in her plea to get together for Jessica's sake, and although I was still skeptical, I was willing to understand what caused the change in her.

"And about that time, her phone rings and she takes a call and walks into another room. My bedroom of all places where I can't hear her. So, I'm wondering who she's talking to that is so private. When she returns, her face is flushed, and I ask if she's all right. She says, 'Sure,' but I sense something is off. So I say, 'Do you mind my asking why you had to leave the room for that conversation?' She tells me it was private.

"I say, 'If our marriage has any chance of working again, we shouldn't be having private conversations. Ones we can't trust to share with each other.' Wouldn't you agree, Mary?"

I do agree with Mike but I don't say anything, waiting for his next words.

"Mary, it isn't going to work with Kimberly. I'm sure that was Lance on the phone, and I can't imagine dealing with his calls if I return to Kimberly. As much as I love Jessica, I can't agree to that arrangement. I never did find out her motivation for wanting to get back together. I think she and Lance had a falling out and now he's trying to make up. So I asked her to leave, and we would proceed with our court date. She stormed out the door. I've been wanting to call you for some time—" he hesitates.

"It's okay. Had you called sooner I might not have been as receptive. I've had some time to think now and…"

He interrupts me. "I have to say one more thing. Even if you and I hadn't met, I would not have agreed to go back to Kimberly. You are not the one keeping me from being with Jessica."

"Thank you for telling me that," I say and feel some relief.

He says, "So do you think we could go to dinner? Sort of start over?"

"Sure, but I'd rather start where we left off instead of over."

"Let me check my work schedule. It will post tomorrow.

"That sounds good." I hang up the phone and call Rosetta immediately.

The minute she picks up, I say, "My heart said 'Yes' and so did my mouth. We're going out again."

Violetta Armour

TEDDY

I want to tell Mindy about my meeting with Mike. These days I want to tell Mindy everything. I stop by her house, and she's down in the basement again.

"More rocks?" I ask. "Still planting those around town?" I pick up a big one that reads, *Hope.*

"Where are you going to leave this one?"

"Not sure. I'm actually working on a little scavenger hunt." An open notebook sits in front of her. I like the way her little lips pucker up on the end of the pencil eraser she's chewing on. She rarely wears lipstick, which surprises me as much as she loves color. But she makes up for it with the clothes she wears. Today an orange jumpsuit like a construction worker might wear. Where does she find these outfits? Especially in such small sizes. Maybe in the preschool costume room where they play dress-up?"

"If you found this poem where would you go?" She reads it to me.

> *See the ponies with big black manes*
> *Fancy beaded saddles, golden reins*
> *Instead of riding forward into the night*
> *They go up and down to kids' delight.*

I think for a minute and then I say, "That's easy. A merry-go-round."

"And where would you find one in Middleburg?"

"What is this? A test? At the amusement park we went to last year."

"Okay, you pass." She tosses me one of the little rocks, which I try to catch but drop.

She laughs and calls me Klutz while we both bend down to pick it up. Our heads bump and when we look up, her pixie face is mere inches from mine. I have this urge to kiss each freckle. How ridiculous that would be as she has so many. I hand her the rock and we both straighten up.

"I wanted to tell you about my talk with Mike. I went to the fire station."

"Oh yeah? Did he think it was a good idea? To have that many candles in a bookstore?"

"Mainly we talked about him taking Mom to dinner the night we sneak the customers into the store. Can you keep a secret?"

"I love secrets. And yes, of course I can. Tell me one."

"Mike isn't divorced yet, and so Mom said she won't see him until he is."

"Oh, no. That's terrible." Mindy's brow furrows. "They're nice together, don't you think? I've been in the bookstore when he's there."

"I haven't seen them together much, but I like the idea of Mom having a friend. Especially a fireman. They're cool."

"Oh, you just want a ride on the fire engine," Mindy says.

"Wouldn't you?"

"Sure, or slide down the pole. There is a pole, isn't there? Can I go with you if you go back there?" Her eyes light up at the thought of it.

"Getting back to Mom and Mike. He's going to ask if she'll have dinner with him one more time. Hope it works or we'll have to go to Plan B. I guess Rosetta and James could take Mom to dinner."

"Mike would be better," she says.

"I agree."

Mindy picks up her phone and looks at the time. "Sorry to run, but I'm supposed to be online now."

"Oh, with that guy. That Lucky guy?"

"Yeah, we're brainstorming some ideas for Jeopardy. We might even get together for a live meeting instead of a virtual one."

I say, "Sure," and follow her upstairs. I leave her house feeling *unlucky* and thinking that *Hope* rock might be perfect for me. I hope Mindy doesn't like this guy more than she likes me.

Violetta Armour

Teddy

We're all set for the night of the *Save the Store* scheme. Everyone is in place and I call Mom, who is at the at the corner restaurant with Mike. I fake an emergency.

"Mom, I'm closing up and noticed some water on the floor in the children's section. Do you want to check it out?"

"Guess I'd better. I'll be right down. Mike and I just finished dinner."

I say to Mindy, "So far so good. Plan on schedule."

We quickly light everyone's candle at breakneck speed. It's like Christmas Eve in church with one person tipping their candle to light the next one. I put the CD in, and Mindy's ready to hit the play button the minute Mom arrives. We have about five minutes and hope our candles don't burn down before she arrives.

My heart is racing. I want this so much for Mom, who's put her heart and soul into this store. She loves it so much—the books, the customers, Footnote, the kids…"

I hear the sound of the key turning in the front door, which I locked to avoid her surprising us. The lights are out, with only the glow of thirty-three—I counted them—candles, customers holding them in two rows down the center aisle. Mindy hits the CD button and LeAnn Rimes' crystal clear voice comes on with "You Light Up My Life" as she enters the store with Mike a few steps behind her.

She looks stunned. "What…?"

Mindy lowers the music a touch, and I step out from behind the greeting-card rack. "Mom, we're all here tonight to show you how much your store means to this community. It needs to stay open no matter how many big stores come near. Here's some of the reasons why your customers will remain loyal."

I turn to the first person in line and nod.

She walks toward Mom. "Mary, when that special book I wanted for my mother's eightieth birthday was out of print, you did a special search and found it. It was the highlight of her day."

Next in line, "Thanks to your *Goosebump* parties for boys on Saturday mornings, Ricky is reading every night. His teacher can't believe his improvement."

Next, a couple walks up together. "Mary, we met at your Saturday-night-singles book club, and we've been dating ever since."

Next, "Mary, one night I was out for my evening walk. I wandered into your store with no purse or money on me. I saw the sequel to a book I've been waiting for, and you said, 'Take it home. You can pay me later. You come in here all the time. I trust you.' That trust and kindness convinced me that I would be your customer and cheerleader forever."

Next, "When our adopted daughter, Dannee, turned thirteen, she wanted to know about her birth parents. You found the perfect book for our search that led us to them. This discovery has made so many people happy."

A burly guy is next. The candle looks tiny in his big hand. "Mary, your book club for Men Only is awesome. My wife thinks it's kind of sexy that I read in bed each night." We hear snickers.

One by one, step by step, they come forward with their stories and praise.

Mom's face radiates in the glow of the candles. Mike stands behind her with a supportive hand on her back.

When all have come forward, Mike cautions everyone to be sure their candles are out. I turn on the lights. Mindy hits the play button, and Kool and the Gang are belting out *Celebration.* through the speaker.

There's laughing and clapping and Baba says, "Come eat. I make delicious baklava for this special night."

MARY

I am astonished. I look around the candlelit room, the glow of beautiful smiles and shining eyes. Teddy, Mindy, Rosetta and James. Luther, Marletta and Baba. Even the girls are here. Cathy and Ruby, their little hands holding their candles high enough to be on the same level as the adults. Ruby stretches on her tiptoes to reach higher. Our eyes connect, and her joyous smile with the front teeth missing brings a smile to my lips.

Mike's hand rests on my back, firm and steady. I can hardly catch my breath when he whispers in my ear, "Just breathe. Take a deep breath."

And I do. When the first person walks toward me with her story, I take it in and it resonates somewhere deep inside me. I look beyond her at the rows of books. So many wonderful stories line those shelves, but tonight there is no story as beautiful as this one.

As the celebration continues, we hug each other and enjoy Baba's baklava and other treats. Then Teddy and Mindy surround me.

Mindy asks, "Did you like it? Will it convince you to keep your store open? You have to. You can see they all want you to."

"Was this your idea—you two?"

They beam at each other. Teddy says, "I have to give Mindy the credit. She thought of it."

"But you made it happen. We're a pretty good team, aren't we?" She punches Teddy's shoulder like she's one of the guys.

I read Teddy's face. He wants more than a punch. He wants a hug. Instead, he smiles and says, "We're a great team, Mindy."

Before he can say anything else, Mindy takes Ruby and Cathy by the hand. "Come on, I'll read you a story."

When everyone is gone and the store is put back together, Mike and

I stroll to the restaurant where our cars are parked. He walks me to mine, and I lean against the door before I unlock it.

"Well, this wasn't exactly what I had planned for tonight," he says, as he leans against the door with both arms above me.

"I suppose you were in on this too?" I ask.

"I suppose. But that wasn't the real reason I asked you to go to dinner."

"Oh? And what was the real reason? You wanted some Mexican food?"

He laughs. "I wanted us to pick up, as you said, where we left off. I wanted to talk to you across the table, to make your blue eyes laugh a bit, and brush your hand while you're reaching for a chip... and even get a hug good-night."

"I guess that's still a possibility," I say as I lean into him, my heart beating against his chest.

He leans down and wraps his arms around me and I feel so comforted. "This feels as good as all those candle talks," I say.

"I will take that as a compliment," he says. "They were awesome."

"I'm on such a high right now, I could fly all the way home."

"Why don't you let me drive you home? We can get your car tomorrow."

"That's a good idea," I say.

"Maybe I could come in for a nightcap?"

"You are full of good ideas tonight," I say as we walk to his car.

MARY

The Christmas spirit is in the air at the bookstore. The windows are decorated with gift books and garland and holiday decals. Even Footnote is sporting a new red collar, but we aren't telling him that there's a jeweled bling-bling on it that only a girl cat should wear. We've switched our music from Mozart and Enya to Bing Crosby's "White Christmas" and Johnny Mathis's "O Holy Night," which is playing now. I stay with the more traditional music, figuring the radio stations will feature the newest releases.

I'm restocking the shelves when Mindy comes up to me.

"Mary, look." She rolls her eyes in the direction of the Kids Corner.

I look but don't see anything unusual. "What?"

She takes me by the elbow and leads me closer. A little girl and an old man with a white beard sit in the corner. She's showing him the cover of a chapter book.

I look at Mindy with an expression that I hope conveys, "So?"

She pulls me out of earshot and whispers, "He's perfect. You said you wished we had a good Santa for Santa Storytime."

I look back at him. "Mindy, you're absolutely right. His beard is snow white. He even has rosy cheeks."

"Yeah, kids can spot those fake beards…and that's when they yank on them. Do you know him?" Mindy asks.

"No, I don't recognize him."

Then a lady I do know walks by. She says, "Hey, Mary."

"Lisa. How are you?" Then I make the connection.

"Is that your Emma?" I point to the children's section. "My gosh, she's grown so much I didn't even recognize her."

"Just turned nine. She brought my dad in because she knows he'll buy her any book she wants."

"Of course." I smile. "He looks so kind. Um, Lisa, I was wondering. Do you think he might agree to play Santa for an afternoon? We want to do a Santa Storytime. I was going to rook my brother-in-law into it, but with his dark hair and tan complexion, it might not be believable."

"I could ask him."

"Would you? We'd give him some books for Emma as a thank you."

"That should clinch the deal."

A few minutes later Lisa returns. He said yes."

I grab a notepad and jot the date and times. "I'll read some stories, and if he'd stay a while, the parents would love to take photos. It has to be better than fighting the lines at the mall. He's so authentic. Thank you, Lisa. And we'll rent the Santa suit."

Lisa checks to see that Emma's out of earshot and whispers to me over the counter. "Emma still believes. I'll have to tell her Papa is being Santa's helper. Papa is a pretend Santa."

As they leave the store, I shake Papa's hand. "Thank you so much."

He nods his head with a shy smile.

The sense of Christmas joy is starting to spread through me. Surely this year will be easier than the last one was, our first without Stan. I can only hope so.

The day of Santa Storytime arrives, and the children pile in and settle in a circle at Santa's feet. The Santa suit we rented came with a big black buckle and wire-rim glasses. It included the beard, which we didn't need. Emma sits close to the foot of her grandfather's chair.

At one o'clock, I ring a little bell. A few more children appear. I'm wearing a red dress and white apron with a ruffled white cap like Mrs. Claus. I sit in the chair beside Santa and read a few favorites. *Polar Express, The Littlest Angel*.

The last book is a large version of *The Night Before Christmas*. As I hold it up, one little girl says, "Let Santa read it."

"Wonderful idea," I agree and hand the book to Santa. "Would you?" I ask.

I place the book in his hands and his rosy cheeks turn even redder. He opens it to the first page and stares at the words. The children wait.

Suddenly, Emma jumps up and stands beside her grandfather.

"Papa…I mean Santa." She points to the wire-rim glasses resting on his nose. "These are not your own reading glasses. Let me read and you can hold up the book to show all the pictures."

As Emma reads, "And what to their wondering eyes should appear…" I notice that Santa follows each word with his index finger and is mouthing the words silently, appearing to stumble on a few. My face turns hot with shame.

"And to all a good night," Emma reads, and Santa repeats in his deep voice with a slight accent, "And to all a good night." He puts his arm around Emma's waist and pulls her close to him.

I hand him a bag, which contains little *Golden Books* for him to give each child. The sound of the mothers' cameras clicking as each child sits on Santa's lap.

I pull Emma aside. "I am so sorry if I embarrassed your papa. I didn't know…"

She looks me straight in the eye. "That's okay, Miss Mary." She speaks softly, "I'm teaching him to read. It's something we do together. He reads good in German, but he only has two books. He reads them over and over. If I teach him to read in English, he'll have so many more to choose from. I love my books and would be sad if I didn't have them."

"That's a wonderful thing you are doing, Emma," I say as I pull a wisp of stray blond hair off her cheek. A better way to thank Santa might be to order some German books for him.

That night as I go through my nightly routine of closing the store, shelving books that have been left out and balancing the cash drawer, I am pleased with the receipt total. This is the month that might make a difference in our first-year-of-operation profit.

Then I think of Emma and Papa. The sales of the day please me, but not as much as what I witnessed. I saw the true spirit of Christmas in a little girl's eyes.

At this moment I feel Stan's absence keenly. I want to share this moment with him. I turn off the music and the lights and step onto Main Street, which looks so festive. The street lamps reflect a dusting of snow fluttering like the teardrops in my heart.

TEDDY

George asks me if I'll come over and help him decorate his tree. When I get there he has a tree already in a stand and a few boxes on the floor with decorations.

He says, "I haven't put up a tree for years. Not since the Mrs. is gone. I go to my daughter's in California for Christmas Day so I ask myself, "Who's going to see my tree?""

"So what's different about this year?" I ask.

"What's different?" He smiles at me. "I guess it's you Teddy. You make this house seem like a home again, taking time to come talk to an old geezer like me."

I want to tell him how much I like being here too but I think he's embarrassed about what he said and is now bent over a box of decorations.

"Here's what I'm looking for." He pulls an angel out of the box. "By gosh, I think you're tall enough to put this angel on without my getting a ladder."

He hands it to me and I place it on the top branch. We stand back and admire her and then we start adding ornaments. George has a few stories about where each one came from. A special vacation. A home-made one from a grandchild. A very old one he remembers as a child. And then he tells me about childhood Christmas' at the ranch.

"There was a true spirit of giving in that old mountain community. Sharing what you had with the neighbors, giving homemade gifts to one another, taking food to the widows in the area.

"We never had a shortage of beef or elk in our freezer," he says. "To supplement our income, Dad and a neighbor started an elk hunting-guide service. Each city-slicker hunter paid one-thousand dollars for a five-day hunt. That was a lot of money back then. We guaranteed the hunter would get shots at the elk, but of course we couldn't guarantee success. Besides, most of them couldn't hit the side of a barn even if they were inside with the doors closed.

"On a typical day of the hunt, Dad would get us boys up while it was still dark, and we would saddle all the dudes' horses while Dad cooked breakfast. We loved doing this. A lot of work, but a heck of a lot more fun than going to school. We'd leave the campsite on Buzzard Creek while it was still dark and lead the hunters to various sure spots where the dudes could see elk, since we'd made a sweep to drive them there.

"One of two things would happen. It would sound like World War III, when we got to the hunters, and they'd be jumping up and down like little kids, saying, 'Let's do it again' even if they hadn't hit any elk.

"Or we'd steer a bunch of elk up through a saddle where Dad had left the hunters and told them the elk would be coming as soon as it was daylight. Then we wouldn't hear a thing. When we reached where the hunters were supposed to be, they'd vanished. We finally found them around the bend, and the dudes said they'd decided another place to wait was better. Dad always muttered, 'Dumber than a box of rocks.'"

"You said he took them up through a saddle. Like a horse's saddle?"

George laughs. "Not exactly. Saddle is another name for a gap in the mountains where animals can pass through." He goes on. "Early afternoon Dad would take the hunters back to camp, and we would finish field dressing the elk we got, pack it back to camp, and hang it in the trees to cool out. Some of the men went back to camp, but the true sportsmen would stay and help us take care of their meat. Some of the hunters only wanted the antlers, so Dad would give the meat to some of the poor folks or widows in the area."

"Sounds like your Dad and my Baba had a lot in common, wanting to keep the world fed."

"And that's a good thing, isn't it?" George says as he takes another big spoonful of the stuffed peppers Baba sent for him.

When it's time to leave, night has fallen and the tree looks pretty with the lights.

"Thanks for coming over, Teddy." George says at the doorway.

I want to tell George how much he means to me but don't know how to say it. Then I remember one of the ornaments I hung. I walk over to the tree and pull it off. I hand it to George.

"I like what this one says." It's silver and in the shape of an angel. The words engraved on it are, *Sometimes angels are disguised as friends.*

I give the "old geezer" a big hug and go out the door.

MARY

On December twelfth, we find a package at the front door of the bookstore when we arrive to open. It says, *On the first day of Christmas, your true friends say to you. I hope the joy will last all year through. Bet You can't catch me.* And there is a twelve-inch gingerbread-man cookie smiling at us.

The next day, another package sits at the front door. *On the second day of Christmas, your true friends bring to you, two turtledoves.* There's a box of Turtles candy...yum. We put it in beside the coffee for our customers, along with the note.

The notes and gifts continue for the next ten days, and soon we set up a table to display them. Customers often return mainly to see what we received that day. We don't know who's leaving them but we suspect a few. Those we confront, of course, deny it vehemently.

On the twenty-fourth of December, our busiest day of the year, there's no package at the front door. We are disappointed as we can't wait to get to the store each day to see what our surprise is.

About noon, in walks one of our favorite families, The Davidson's—Roberta, Karl, and their children, ages ten and eight. The scent of warm pumpkin and sugar floats through the door with them from the huge cake pan they carry. Perched on top of the cake is a little brown Christmas teddy bear and a note. *On the 12th day of Christmas, your true friends bring to you—one Teddy bear—who couldn't keep up with the Lords of Leaping. Merry Christmas!*

Indeed, it's a merry one. Although we shared all the previous gifts with our customers, we selfishly stash this one in the office, and in between sales, we run back and eat heaping spoonfuls of the pumpkin cake. It fills both our tummies and our hearts.

January 2001
TEDDY

I call Mindy on Saturday morning, and her mother says she's out. "I thought she said she was going somewhere with you."

I don't want to worry her mother so I say, "Oh, yeah, we were going to meet at the bookstore." The bookstore is my next stop in case she's working today. She often works a few hours each Saturday.

"Hey, Mom, is Mindy here?"

"No, is she supposed to be?"

"I just wondered. Is she scheduled to work anytime today?"

"No, I asked her if she wanted to pick up a few hours, and she said no, but she could come in tomorrow. I have her down for two to five."

"Hmmm…did she by chance mention anything about why she couldn't work?"

Knowing her, it could be something like working on her pet rock project—hiding rocks throughout Middleburg—or delving into some Jeopardy research. Who knows where?

"No, she didn't say," Mom says, and turns to ring up a sale.

Something is nagging at me about Mindy. Why would she tell her mother she was going to be with me? Then I remember that she didn't want her parents to know about this Lucky guy and what if she's meeting him, using me as a foil.

Something doesn't feel right about this. I need to find her. *Think, Teddy, think. Where would Mindy go?* Knowing her, it would be some place unusual. Not a typical meeting place like a normal person, like a coffee shop or a McDonalds.

The last time we talked about him, she said he wanted to meet her, and because he was such a brainiac, she was going to make it tricky. He would need to figure out the clue. I should have nipped it then and there. But I didn't know they had set a day and time to do it.

Okay, so where would the clues be? I can't go back to her house to look. Her mother thinks she's with me. I drive around Middleburg, past the school, cruise down Main Street. I drive past the cemetery—now that's something Mindy might suggest. I pass through the gates and follow the familiar route, driving slowly on the gravel road. I park in my usual spot and walk towards Dad's gravestone, all the time looking around for signs of Mindy.

"Hey, Dad," I say as I pass his stone. "I'm on a wild goose chase here. Looking for a little redhead with lots of freckles and probably wearing some wild colors. She would sure be a bright spot here."

I think about all the Saturdays we spent together. Building that snowman here for Dad, making snow angels in Patriot Park, climbing the historic fort the first time I told her about Dad, and there was the trip to the amusement park and riding the horses on the carousel when it was closed. Something triggers...something she said last time we were together. About a merry-go-round. The poem.

I thought the poem was about a place to hide one of her pet rocks where someone would find it next summer. But what if that was the clue for creepy Lucky? The amusement park is on the edge of town. Deserted this time of year.

I run back to my car. "Hey, Dad, I gotta go. Love you." I jump in my car and head to the edge of town.

MARY

Mike and I are at his house with our new 2001 calendars. I have a new journal for long-range plans and pipe dreams that I let the girls help me decorate with stickers. I didn't let them so much as they assumed it was okay to do so, and I didn't have the heart to curtail their enthusiasm. I'm glad because now I can see their crafty designs daily, and remember the fun session we had at Baba's kitchen table.

Mike has made a fresh pot of coffee, and we're ready to help each other map out our goals, some separately and some together. It begins in a positive mode with some simple thoughts. He wants to work out more faithfully. I want to read books in a genre I don't normally choose, perhaps sci fi.

Then I feel myself becoming nostalgic as I look ahead into April and the family week we spent at the beach. A wave of fresh grief passes through me—something I haven't felt for some time. There are, of course, twinges always, like the night I walked out of the bookstore after Santa Claus and Emma, something I wanted to share with Stan. And the holidays were daily reminders of the traditions we established in our marriage. Some with the kids and some the two of us before the children came. Each ornament we put on the tree held a memory.

I try to remember what the grief counselor said. Healing happens when you can change the way you think about painful incidents. Try to turn it around where you are saying to yourself, I am so grateful to have had this moment rather than the sadness that it now brings. Sometimes it works for me. Not always.

Mike says, "Hey, do I sense that this goal-setting is making you unhappy? You look sad."

"I was thinking of Stan," I said.

Mike, early on, has encouraged me to talk about Stan as much as I need to. This was one quality that endeared me to him. That I could be open and honest with my feelings, but also in some small way, he might come to know Stan.

I said at the time, "You can talk about Kimberly all you want to, as well."

He laughed. "Probably best I don't."

"Oh, there must have been good times. When you first met and fell in love. In love enough to have Jessica."

He smiled and kissed me gently. "You're a special lady. To not be jealous of a first wife, but to help me remember her good qualities."

Today, thinking about that conversation and now feeling sad about setting goals for the coming year without Stan, the tears unexpectedly flow.

Mike sets a box of tissues beside me. I blow my nose and say to Mike, who simply lets me cry. "It's not so much about what I am missing with Stan. It's about what Stan is missing with the kids. They're growing up so quickly. I'm sorry for the outburst. This was supposed to be fun."

"You don't have to apologize." He rubs the top of my head gently. "Hang on a minute. I'll be right back." He returns carrying a book with a sheet of paper marking a page. "I read this the other day and meant to show it to you. This might be the right time."

I silently read the passage he has marked. *This is what it must be like to be married to a widow. You give her bandages for her wounds. You offer comfort when memories sneak up, and she cries for what looks like no reason. When she reminisces about the past, you don't remind her of the things she has chosen not to recall.*

Mike says, "I'm not implying that we are married, but I want you to know if this is how you feel sometimes, I want to understand…and it's okay. It's all okay."

I simply say, "Thank you." Then I turn to the first page of my new journal—my gratitude page. It's at the beginning, so I can be reminded each day of what to be thankful for. I have the children's names, of course, Baba, my good health and the bookstore. Under all those I add, *Grateful for Mike, who isn't a doctor but always seems to have his first-aid kit ready for me.*

Just writing his name in there makes me feel better. I glance at him and say, "Grief is such a peculiar emotion. Sometimes it comes at you so unexpectedly out of nowhere. And sharp, like a paper cut...it often surprises you."

"But you can put a Band-Aid on the paper cut," he says. "So how do you turn it around when that happens?"

"Good question. Sometimes I wallow in it, but that seems to be happening less and less. Or something goofy the kids will say or do is often the jolt I need." Mike's compassionate smile encourages me to say, "And you. You are a wonderful antidote."

"Are you saying I'm goofy?"

"Oh, no doubt about that."

We both laugh, and another grieving moment has dissolved, replaced with a lightness in my heart. A lightness that is so welcome.

Mike covers my right hand resting on the table. I look down and see my wedding and engagement ring still on my left hand. It's time.

"Mike, in fairness to you, I should take one more step in the new year."

He looks at me with raised brows.

I smile at him. "A lot of relationships begin when someone puts a ring on their finger. This relationship deserves a new beginning by taking a ring off." I say this as I wriggle the rings off my finger. "You've been so patient and understanding. And kind."

Mike takes my hands in his and it feels right.

Teddy

As I approach the amusement park, a car horn beeps intermittently. It gets louder as I drive close to the entrance. I park my car and run toward the sound. There's a junky rusted car and Mindy's bike beside it.

I race to the car and look in the window. A man is sprawled over Mindy on the front seat. Her legs are kicking up, one leg kicking the horn and she's trying to pound on the window behind her with one free hand.

I try to open the door but it's locked. I bang on the window, and a scrawny man with a mangy beard looks up, startled. He jumps off Mindy, swings wide the car door on the passenger side and pushes her out. She tumbles at my feet and I drag her away from the car which he is starting. He takes off.

I bend over Mindy who is sobbing. I should get the license plate, but I can't let go of her while she's crying. We're both on our knees now and she wraps her arms around my waist so tightly.

"Teddy, I was so stupid. You warned me. You told me to be careful. Why didn't I listen to you?"

I hold her close but then pull away a bit and stare at her. "You are okay, aren't you? He didn't…". I glance down at her clothes to see if she is fully dressed. "Did he hurt you?"

"No, he didn't hurt me, but what a creep. Trying to put his mouth on mine. His breath was awful. So disgusting."

I hold her close to me, and she nestles her little red head into my chest. I keep stroking the top of her head and let her.

"Teddy, please don't tell my parents."

I'm torn as to how to answer. We need to report this guy somehow. Why didn't I get his license?

"I'm so embarrassed. Please, don't tell a soul."

"We need to tell the police. He's a predator on young girls."

She keeps crying, so I postpone this discussion until later. We throw Mindy's bike in the trunk of my car and I drive her home.

"Do you want me to stay with you a while?"

"Thanks, but I need to take a shower and scrub that scum off me."

"Mindy, I don't want to make you feel worse than you do, but why did you get in the car with him? I don't understand."

"I didn't know it was him. I thought he would come on a bike too. When I got there the car was there and this guy was leaning against it and he said, "I think I'm lost. Do you know your way around here?" He had a map in his hand and his front door was still open. He didn't look dangerous. Sort of old and confused.

"So I walked over to him and he was showing me the map and then before I knew it, he grabbed me and threw me across the front seat. He said, 'Oh, I'm lucky alright. You're even cuter than I thought you would be.'"

She starts crying again and I just hold her.

"I'm so sorry, Teddy. So sorry. I was so stupid."

I don't know what else to say so I keep saying, "It's alright. As long as you're alright. You'll feel better after you shower and if you want to talk or for me to come back, I will."

She starts hiccupping between the sobs and then we both laugh a little.

"Don't tell me you're drunk too?" I say jokingly. Then, "I'm not trying to make light of it, Mindy. I just want you to feel okay. Okay?"

She nods her head up and down and the hiccups subside. I walk her to the front door and say, "Scrub hard …and then call me. Promise?'

"I promise," she says and walks in.

On the drive home, my anger about that creep builds. As I pass the church, the sign says *Anger is one letter short of danger*. I feel like doing something dangerous but don't know what to do. Like the sayings in the Book of Life always hit home for me so many times on a particular day, now the sign does too. Life is a mystery to me.

I need to find a way to report this incident, yet keep my promise to Mindy.

I go to Uncle Dan's the next day and vow him to secrecy. When he agrees, I ask him how we can handle this without jeopardizing Mindy's trust. He writes down Mindy's email and says I should try and get the creep's email and the dates of their exchanges as best I can. He says he will find a way to report it. Having a daughter himself, he is also furious to think of the predators out there, preying on innocent girls.

The next day Uncle Dan calls me and says this is more of a common practice than we ever imagined. There is a complete division that handles this cybercrime, and they will do all they can to track him down.

Dan says, "You know, I'm sort of surprised that Mindy let this happen. I know she's a smart girl."

"She's brainy, Uncle Dan, but she's not what you might call street smart. Mindy's pretty naive in a lot of ways." Thinking of Mindy's trusting nature, I get angry about the whole situation again and angry at myself for not following my hunch that Lucky might have been a creep. It makes me want to hold her close to me again.

MARY

The new big bookstore is opening this weekend. I want to go, but I'm afraid I'll get so depressed. Should I go alone? Should I take Mike with me? Should I go at all? It's not like I've never been in a bookstore before. But this is different. This is the competition. And what if I run into my customers?

I can hardly blame them for looking, as I would be doing the same. But I won't, of course, be buying anything as they might. I'll hang out at one of the tables in the coffee shop. Watch the traffic go by.

I screw up my courage and take the plunge. I drive there mid-afternoon, which might be a slow time, park my car a long distance from the front door to walk off my jitters and take a deep breath before I walk in. The smell of new books is immediate and is enticing and delicious. The music is something classical, and I see that they have a complete music corner.

As I browse through the various sections, I catch myself, out of habit, straightening the books on a shelf or facing a book out that someone has set down. *What am I doing? This isn't my store.*

The children's section is huge and has a large selection of toys as well as books. Adjacent is a section on games both for children and adults. I'm mentally making notes on ways I can expand my inventory to compete. One minute I am inspired, the next I'm despondent. It's a bit overwhelming.

I saunter to the café section where I spot a few of my customers having coffee and what looks like some decadent pastry concoction. I don't want to make them uncomfortable, so I slip out of the store. Taking a deep breath of fresh air, I decide to bring Mike with me next time. Someone to lean on. If I have the courage to return, that is.

TEDDY

I hand Mindy a box, which I gift-wrapped. It looks like a four-year-old did it.

"Here's something that might help you get ready for Jeopardy finals. I thought long and hard about this and what you might need the most."

"You didn't have to get me anything. It's not even my birthday. What is it?"

"Open it, silly, and you'll find out."

She rips into the paper. "What in the world?" She pulls the items out of a basket. Fresh blueberries, nuts, a can of tuna fish, raw broccoli, a bunch of carrots, avocados, a bag of coffee grounds, and some green stems with little spikes.

"Everything in this box has magical powers, so they say—*they* being that elusive body of know-it-alls."

"*They* say magical?" Mindy asks.

"*They* say that all these items are brain food. Except for the plant. That's rosemary, which is good for memory retention. Can't just know all this stuff...gotta remember it too."

Mindy keeps touching all the items and shaking her head. She must think it's a stupid gift. "You don't believe it? Don't like it?" I ask.

"Like it? I love it! This is the nicest gift I've ever received. And you know what else I love?"

I slap my forehead. "Dark chocolate. I forgot the dark chocolate."

"Are you listening to me, Teddy? Yes, I love chocolate, but even more than that...more than this—" She points to the box. "More than anything, Teddy Kostoff..." She peers up at me, "I love YOU."

Then she stands on her tippy-toes and pulls my face down close to hers and kisses me right on the mouth.

Of course, our first kiss would be over a box of brain food. And right now, my brain is popping on all cylinders…or neurons, or whatever they are called. Mindy *loves* me. Mindy loves *me*. Mindy loves me.

Rosetta

I call Mary and relay Luther's message of wanting to meet with her to talk about Stan. She responds in such a positive manner it makes me wonder why we didn't do it sooner.

"Rosetta, that's a great idea. I always welcome a chance to talk about Stan."

We meet at my house where James has prepared some wonderful snacks for us. Crostini with tomatoes, feta and pine nuts.

"For starters, Luther, I can tell you that Stan would have loved this appetizer. He might have complained as usual about not getting a good tomato in Arizona. Whenever we visited Indiana in the summer, the first thing he wanted to eat was a simple tomato sandwich on white bread, lots of mayo, and slices of deep red tomatoes from his mother's garden."

Luther laughs and says, "That's exactly the kind of things I want to know. Specifics. The little things. What were some of his other favorites?"

"Hmm...I guess the usual. Steaks, medium rare, but he liked the end cut of a prime rib. Cheeseburgers and tuna melts."

"So far, all my favorites too," Luther says and turns to me. "Mom, you've had medical training. Are taste buds acquired or something in our DNA?"

I laugh. "Nurses' training didn't cover that area, and DNA findings are relatively new. It would be interesting to explore. I've heard stories of people who get heart transplants and often their taste buds change to reflect what the donor liked. Don't know if there's any truth to that or not." I shrug and sip my wine, enjoying this moment with Luther and Mary. Her eyes light up when she talks about Stan.

"How was his health? Anything I should be aware of?" Luther asks.

I say, "Now that's a good question. It's one kids who are adopted often wish they knew about their biological parents."

Mary takes a moment to answer. "He was prone to sinus infections and had sinus surgery one year to remove polyps. That gave him a lot of relief, but the doctor said he might need it again at some point if they returned. Other than that, he was healthy. Liked to work out at the gym, and he played half-court basketball at the Y with a bunch of guys every Saturday.

"He was getting into cycling since it's a year-round sport in Arizona. If you like to sweat, that is. Didn't sound like fun to me when the temperature hits 115. His cycling buddies rode at daybreak on the weekends or before work. He donated blood a few times a year because they said he had a rare blood type that was in demand."

Luther says, "Must have been O negative. Same as mine."

"I have some home movies if you'd like to see them. They're on VCR tapes," Mary says.

Luther's face lights up. "I would love that." Then he adds somewhat wistfully, "It would be nice to watch them with Teddy."

Mary and I look at each other.

You're right, Luther." Mary says. "We need to tell Teddy. Sometime soon. I don't know why I'm finding it so hard to do."

"Do you know what's holding you back, Mary?"

"No, I don't think he'll disapprove, but I'm afraid he'll be angry that we didn't tell him sooner. Like when I first found out. So the longer I wait, the more that fear increases. Doesn't make sense, does it?"

"Actually it does. We need to do this soon. And we should tell Baba," I add.

Mary nods. "First thing she'll want to do is put more meat on Luther's bones."

We all laugh, then Mary says, "I promise you that we'll have this conversation soon."

TEDDY

Three carloads are headed to Indianapolis for the Jeopardy Teen Tournament Finals. Mindy's family, James, Rosetta, Dr. Stone, Mom, Ruby, Cathy and myself. Baba wanted to stay home and Mike is on the next forty-eight hours at the station.

We arrive the day before and check into a nice hotel near the taping studio. As we gather in the lobby to check in, Mom says to all of us, "You know, Mindy, the fact that the finals are being held in Indianapolis so we could all be here to cheer you on tells me fortune is on your side. I think it's an omen of good things to come."

We have an early dinner so Mindy won't be up too late, but she insists on checking out the indoor pool after dinner and then decides to swim.

"I think some exercise will help me sleep better," she says.

We all agree, so us four kids go back to the rooms for our suits and the adults sit around the pool watching us play Marco Polo and other ridiculous water games. I put Cathy on my shoulders and Mindy heists Ruby on hers, but Ruby weighs almost as much as Mindy and they topple easily. On the way back to our rooms, Mindy spots the vending machine and says, "Wait here." The girls run to our room and I wait there for Mindy. She returns with several dollars and starts feeding them into the slot.

"In case I have a snack attack in the middle of the night," she claims. She pushes the buttons mainly for candy bars as she turns to me. "Chocolate. Remember, you said I needed dark chocolate in your care package."

"Yeah, but not every candy bar ever made." I say.

"Okay, I'll share," she says as she throws me a bag of M and M's. "Share with your sisters, okay?"

When we get to our rooms which are next to each other Mindy and I stand there with our big pool towels wrapped around us. Her curly red hair which is normally going in every direction is still wet, straight and stringy and she looks like a little girl, not someone capable of earning $100,000.00.

I just want to hug this little girl, but I'm trying to figure out how to do that while hanging on to the towel wrapped around me. I decide to let the towel drop and I wrap my arms around her and her wet towel, my M & M's still in hand. I smell the chlorine in her hair and feel all the other candy bars smashed between us in her hands. We both start laughing at our ridiculous stance.

"You know, laughing will help me sleep as much as the swimming did," she says.

"Should I call you in the middle of the night with a joke?" I ask.

She laughs again. "How about one right now?"

"Knock-knock."

"Who's there?"

"Someone."

"Someone who?"

"Someone who thinks you are the bravest person I know. And the cutest…well, maybe not right this minute," I say as I tug on one of her stringy wet locks.

"Is that a joke, Teddy?" About being brave I mean."

"No, Mindy, it's the truth. And you know whatever happens tomorrow, even if it's third place, you are a winner. You do know that don't you?"

She smiles sheepishly. "Are you angling for another candy bar?"

"Angling? What kind of word is that? Are you a fisherman or what?"

We both smile at each other and she shakes her head as if she can't believe this silly conversation we are having.

I take the ends of her towel that is still around her and open it around me so we are both wrapped up in it. I pull her closer with the towel and our wet bodies are touching. I lower my face to hers.

I whisper, "Can I give you a kiss for good-luck tomorrow? I for sure can't do that with the whole family looking on."

She doesn't answer but lifts her sweet face with wet freckles and stringy hair close to my lips and we kiss.

Mindy might win Jeopardy but I feel like I won the jackpot tonight.

The next morning after breakfast we all head to the studio. I think the rest of us are more nervous than Mindy or she is hiding it well. It's a two-day tournament but the taping of both sessions takes place in one day. The contestants and families in the audience are sworn to secrecy of the results until the show airs the following month.

She can barely see over the podium and is clearly the shortest of the three and the only girl. The stage manager offers her a step stool, but she refuses it for fear she will get excited and slip off. Four members of each family can sit in the front row audience. Mindy picks her parents and me and Dr. Stone for all his tutoring help. The rest of our entourage are in the second row behind us.

At the end of the first taping, Mindy is in second place but only trailing first place by three thousand dollars. She will get at least twenty-five-thousand for third place. Second place gets fifty thousand, and a hundred thousand dollars for first.

There's a short break and then they begin round two. Early on in this round, Mindy runs the entire category of Also a Candy Bar with super-quick clicking of her buzzer.

Answer: Athos, Aramis Porrhos. Question: Who are the Three Musketeers?

Answer: A famous street in New York City. Question: What is 5th Avenue?

Answer: A baseball legend. Question: Who is Baby Ruth?

Answer: A little chuckle. Question: What is a Snickers bar?

Answer: A common household pet. Question: What is a Kit-Kat

While we all applaud her running the category she looks right at me as if to say, "See, those candy bars paid off."

I'm hoping this is another one of Mom's good omens.

Then she hits the Daily Double. She has twenty-eight hundred dollars. I'm so nervous she's going to go for it and what if she loses? She'll have zero.

Sure enough she says, "Let's make it a true daily double, Alex."

She looks at me and holds up both hands with fingers crossed. The category is Famous Men from Illinois.

I hope it's an easy one like Abraham Lincoln, but that would be too easy. I can hardly stand to watch her daring move. My stomach is churning and my palms are moist.

Alex Trebek says, "A retail giant who established 250 stores in the U.S., but all recently closed."

Music plays and Mindy looks pensive. Oh my gosh, I can't believe I know this. From my talks with George. I'm clenching my fists wanting so much to magically transfer my brain waves to hers. Say Montgomery Ward, Mindy. Say it.

Time is running out. Alex Trebek says, "Say something, Mindy."

She blurts out, "Marshall Field."

Alex says, "No, I'm sorry, the answer is Montgomery Ward. But it's early in the game. Pick again."

My heart sinks. I told her she was brave and right now I wish she hadn't been.

I know that look she's sporting. It's the same look she had when she told me about Helena in Shakespeare. Helena, little but mighty. Fierce. Mindy has a fierce determination to bounce back and she does. And she seems to be literally bouncing each time she clicks the buzzer. She's worked her way up to first place before Final Jeopardy but only with a $100.00 lead.

Final Jeopardy category is FEMALE VOCALIST. The music plays during the commercial break. Mindy looks out at all of us. Her turquoise braces are gone, and she gives us a big beautiful smile. My tummy does a flip for this courageous person, looking so small on the podium but so big in my heart.

The break is over, and the Final Jeopardy answer flashes on the blue screen and Alex says, "African American Female Vocalist who won both an Emmy and a Grammy as well as a Lifetime Achievement Award. You have thirty seconds contestants."

Mindy's head goes down and she starts writing immediately. This worries me. Mindy is too compulsive. The other two contestants are not writing yet. One is staring out into space with his brow furrowed. Another good omen? The other has his head bent but he is not writing yet.

Think Mindy, think more about your answer. You have more time. But after writing her answer quickly, she puts her chalk down and smiles right at me. No, she's smiling at someone next to me. Dr. Stone. He's smiling too with a thumbs-up sign. Is she so confident in her answer?

How can she be so sure? The other contestants have now also written their answers and the music stops.

The camera focuses on the third-place person's board which reads, Aretha Franklin. Alex Trebek says, "I'm sorry, that's wrong. And what did you wager? All of it, so that leaves zero. So nothing to add to yesterday's score.

Second place person's board flashes up. Diana Ross. Also wrong. He bet zero so he still has money on the board which will add to yesterday's total that was $3000.00 ahead of Mindy.

The camera is on Mindy now, and she is smiling so big. Her chalkboard reads Lena Horne.

Alex Trebek says, Lena Horne is the right answer. Did you bet enough?"

Yes, of course she did. She went for broke and doubled her score. When added to yesterday's total, she wins it all. Jeopardy Teen Tournament Champion.

The celebration begins.

HEADLINE: Small but Mighty Takes It All.

TEDDY

I can't wait to get to George's house and tell him about the Jeopardy finals. "That Mindy," I say, "she's got so much courage to get up there and take a chance like that."

George laughs. "You'd better hang onto that little lady. She will keep your life interesting. Reminds me of my grandmother. Did I tell you about the irrigation ditch she had to defend against the richest rancher in the valley?"

"No, you didn't." I get my soda and stretch out on George's comfy sofa, my legs on the coffee table.

George takes a sip of his coffee and begins. "Grandma owned twenty-five acres, and she shared an irrigation ditch with Harry Palace, who owned over two-hundred-forty acres. The irrigation water was divided up the road a short distance from Grandma's house, and because of the difference in acreage, Harry's opening was ten times wider than Grandma's.

"I often stopped at Grandma's on the way home from school to see if she had any chores. And also because she made the best sugar cookies. One day she told me that she had the most interesting problem. It seems that this large rock kept falling in the ditch, always on Grandma's side. Even when she rolled it downstream below the dividing box, it would roll up stream and block her side again.

I wasn't sure exactly what she meant by that but it meant that she wasn't getting her share of the irrigation water, small as her share was.

Today, Grandma kept watching out the window and all at once she said, "There he is." And when I looked, sure enough, there was Harry Palace at the dividing box. Grandma grabbed her .410 shotgun and said, "Let's go."

I can still see Grandma standing there in front of Harry Palace with her shotgun cradled in the crook of her arm, and I will never forget the way she looked him straight in the eye and quietly said, "Mr. Palace, I hope for your health that this rock never falls into this ditch again." With that she turned and headed home, me trailing behind her.

"She told me later that that rock never did fall into the ditch again. This taught me that when you are right, have the courage to stand up and be counted."

"There's lots of different kinds of courage, isn't there, George?" I say.

"Yep, sometimes it's visible and loud, but the best is the quiet and invisible type of courage—sometimes it's just to not to say a mean-spirited thing when we've been injured or insulted."

I remember the words on the Baptist sign that day. *Words that sink in are whispered, not shouted.*

TEDDY

The rest of our junior year is somewhat anti-climactic after Jeopardy. Our basketball team is rebuilding so we don't go far in the sectionals. Mindy and I spend more time together and even some time with Joe. It makes him happy to see us together, and it's great for the three of us to hang out like old times.

Joe tries to convince Tara to come to Middleburg for the prom, but she's hesitant. Says her parents might let her visit Joe this summer, and Mindy gets on the phone and invites her to stay at her house if that helps the cause.

On prom night I go to Mindy's house a little nervous wearing a tuxedo. I start up her walk and then remember the corsage box sitting on my front seat and go back to the car. Her mother answers the door. "Teddy, you look so handsome." She calls upstairs, "Mindy, Teddy's here."

When Mindy walks down her staircase in a fluffy blue dress looking like a little princess with her red hair in pretty curls instead of going in twenty corkscrew directions, I feel a catch in my heart. I realize I'm gawking and finally remember to hand her the corsage box. She opens it and puts it on her wrist. On the end table is a boutonniere for me and she reaches up to pin it on my lapel. She sticks me with the pin and we both laugh nervously.

"Maybe you better sit down for this," she says and leads me to a dining room chair. When she leans into me to try again, I get a whiff of her hair which reminds me of something sweet, like cotton candy.

Her mother gets her camera and we pose and smile. Her Dad comes in and tells us to have a good time and drive carefully.

When we get in the car, I realize I can't wait to see if she also tastes like cotton candy. I say, "Mindy, there's something on your cheek."

She reaches for the rear-view mirror but I take her hand in mine and with the other one, I touch her cheek.

"Here, let me do it," I say and pretend to flick away the imaginary something with my finger. Leaning close to her I breathe in her scent again and when I put my lips softly on hers I taste her sweetness. She does taste like candy. Very sweet candy.

Then we go to my house for pictures. Ruby and Cathy are peeking out the window waiting for us.

They both start jumping up and down when they see us coming up the walk.

Cathy says, "Mindy, you look like Cinderella." They touch her dress as if it's spun of gold.

Mom and Baba come out of the kitchen and fuss over Mindy too. Mom gets her camera and we pose again.

Baba says, "Oh, Teddy, you so handsome." I think she's wiping a tear from her eye with the edge of her apron. I know she's thinking of Dad and that puts a lump in my throat. I can't look at Mom for fear she'll start tearing up too.

First a catch in my heart, now a lump in my throat. HEADLINE: Prom boy has melt-down.

Before we know it, the school year is coming to an end. We sign yearbooks. Mindy and I reserve a whole page for each other. Then we watch the seniors march to "Pomp and Circumstance" at the City Auditorium.

MARY

The bookstore seems to be holding it's own in spite of the new store in town. We've expanded into some unique lines of gifts and toys related to children's books. Our café is open daily rather than just for special events. We had to do a slight remodel and get a permit to add a small kitchen. Baba's deep-dish pizza is a favorite and brings customers back. So now instead of the store smelling like books and the nice potpourri we had in strategic locations, it smells like Little Italy, but that's not bad. And Baba's phyllo triangles stuffed with feta sell out daily.

I heard that the big chain store's most profitable section is the Godiva chocolate and wonder if I should add a line of chocolates. When I mention that to Teddy he laughs and tells me about the Baptist church sign last week. *Stop trying to make everyone happy. You aren't chocolate.*

The used book corner is growing, offering customers something the chain store doesn't. James says it's more profitable than the new books, so of course we play it up in our ads and it is expanding.

Mindy and Teddy help out but because their hours are limited they both get other jobs for the summer. Teddy at Wendy's which Cathy and Ruby love, since Mom's of employees get free Frosties and that means I get one for each of them too. Mindy works part-time at the library and the one time I saw her in there she had a trail of kids following her like the Pied Piper to the children's reading circle.

Some nights Mindy and Teddy pop in to the bookstore and send me home—they say they'll take care of everything and I trust them to do a good job.

Mindy always says, "No charge, Mrs.K. You don't need to pay Teddy and I to be together. We like playing store."

I have a feeling they probably would like to play house also and I wish Stan were here to have that talk with Teddy. Perhaps Uncle Dan will come to my rescue.

September 2001

TEDDY

Seniors at last. At the end of the first week of school, I pop into Coach Luther's office to shoot the breeze about basketball this year, and Coach Duffy tells me he took some personal days to go to New York City. He said Luther and Marletta were going to a special meeting about the Peace Corps. Sounds like something they would do. I wonder if he's going to introduce a third-world country to the joys of basketball.

The Peace Corps meeting was scheduled at the beautiful World Trade Center on Sept. 11. Now this Sunday, September 15, the entire family is gathered at Rosetta and James' house. It's a somber occasion.

TEDDY

It took Luther and Marletta three days to return to Indiana. All flights in and out of the states were cancelled as soon as the attack occurred. When some of the airlines started flying again on Thursday, Sept.13, they thought the planes would be full with three days of passengers waiting, but in fact, many people were still too frightened to get on a plane. It was no problem for Marletta and Luther to get seats on a flight back to Indianapolis. They landed on Thursday and spent Friday with Marletta's parents.

Now at Rosetta's and James' home, Luther and Marletta sit close to one another on the sofa, their hands and arms entwined. Dr. Stone is beside them. Rosetta and James sit together in an overstuffed chair, half of her on James' lap and the other half resting on the wide armrest. My mom and Mike are in dining room chairs, placed close in the circle, and they hold hands between the chairs.

Mindy and I are on the floor. I'm sitting cross-legged and she sits between my legs. I wrap my arms tightly around her tiny waist and she places her hands on my knees. It's like all of us need to hold onto each other, grateful to be together and paralyzed by the thought of what we might have lost. We all need to be touching one another to assure ourselves that we are here...together.

Baba is home with Cathy and Ruby. Mom thought Luther might describe what they saw and she was afraid it would frighten them. As happy as we are to see Luther and Marletta, the mood is somber and not one of celebration. The unimaginable has occurred for so many families, and we know how fortunate we are to have narrowly escaped such a tragic loss in ours.

We wait quietly. Luther takes a drink of water. He starts to speak. "It is hard to describe...the horror of it..." and then he puts his face in his hands and we hear his sobs.

It is Marletta who continues where he left off, although her voice is shaky. "The Peace Corps meeting we were going to that morning was scheduled for nine o'clock. We checked out of our hotel in Times Square early and left our luggage with the valet. We planned to take a taxi to the hotel after the meeting, pick up our luggage and then continue in that taxi to the airport for our flight home." She pauses for a moment to regain her composure.

"We could have taken a cab to the World Trade Center that morning, but we thought we should experience at least one subway ride before we left New York. When we spoke to the concierge the night before, he told us to take the express line to West Street." She takes a deep breath and glances at Luther. He nods as if telling her to continue.

Marletta takes a drink of water. "We left the hotel to walk to the subway, thinking we had plenty of time to spare. We hadn't gone far when it hit me. I had left our paperwork for the Peace Corps meeting in my carry-on luggage that I'd checked with the doorman. It had our resumes that we were supposed to submit. We couldn't decide if it would be better to be late to the meeting or be on time with no resumes. We decided the resumes were important."

Marletta takes another sip of water and now Luther speaks, "Those forgotten resumes may have saved our lives" He shakes his head. "We became impatient with the valet who was having a casual chat with one of the guests while we waited to get his attention. Finally, we showed him our claim ticket. He walked us to the storage closet and let us pick out our bag and we quickly retrieved the resume folder.

"Then we ran down to the subway and at that point, we knew we should have taken a taxi because there were so many gates and signs and turnstiles we weren't sure which way to go. Another delay and our frustration was growing. Here we were wanting possibly to represent the Peace Corps in a foreign country, and we couldn't even find our way to a meeting in our own country. Who would choose us?"

Marletta says, "Finally, as the express subway sped along—and they weren't kidding when they said express—we glanced at our watches. Eight-forty-five. I remember saying to Luther, 'We might make it. The concierge said the subway will drop us off close to the World Trade Center. Maybe they'll have a little social time before the meeting starts, like with coffee and donuts? And I'm sure they have express elevators.'"

Luther says, "When the subway stopped at West Street, my watch read 8:58. I said to Marletta, 'As soon as we get up to street level, let's make a run for it.'"

"You did," Marletta says. "But when we got to the top of the stairs, instead of seeing the beautiful clear blue sky we had seen earlier that morning, smoke and debris filled the air, paper falling everywhere, complete chaos. People running in all directions. It was like we had stepped out into some kind of war zone. People were shouting, screaming, crying. All were running but constantly looking over their shoulders and up at the sky. We followed their gaze and saw the unimaginable. The World Trade Center was on fire—flames shooting from it and dark smoke billowing around it."

Luther says, "We couldn't take our eyes off it, but we had to keep moving with the crowd of runners or we'd be trampled. Then someone said, 'Oh my God, another plane.' Then the tremendous roar of an engine. Everyone stopped and looked up. A huge plane disappeared into the second tower. I looked at my watch. Three minutes after nine. Yes, we would have definitely missed the start of our meeting, but by the grace of God we wouldn't miss our lives."

Marletta says, "I'll never forget that sound. Like thousands of pieces of shattering glass."

By now all of us in the living room are moved to tears. Marletta goes on. "We haven't slept well since that day. We saw other things that we can't speak of yet. But during those hours, we were awake in the night, and we talked a lot." Marletta looks at Luther.

"We made some decisions. We have no desire to travel far from home as we did before. I look around this room. This is home and where we belong. We want to stay as close to all of you as possible."

Luther smiles now, the first smile since he sat down. "And do you want to tell them what else we decided?"

Marletta blushes. "We don't want to put off having a family. The world is an uncertain place now—a fearful place, but we can't let our fear be stronger than our love. For each other, for our country. If we live in fear, the terrorists win. And what better symbol of love and hope is there than a child?"

Now we are all smiling, Rosetta through her tears. Then Mindy, as usual, makes us all laugh a little, releasing the tension, when she says, "I guess you're not alone in your thinking. Almost four million babies have been born in the U. S. so far this year."

I say. "And you know this because…"

"Because it could have been a Jeopardy category, of course," she says.

I think of a recent sign on the church marquee. *A baby is God's opinion that the world should go on.*

TEDDY

After Luther and Marletta tell their story, we all leave Rosetta's house and go to Baba's for dinner. After the meal, Mom asks Mindy if she'll help Baba clean up in the kitchen and asks me to join her in the living room. Rosetta and Luther are already seated there. Rosetta is holding Dad's yearbook on her lap, smoothing her hand up and down the cover.

She says, "Teddy, I want to show you something." She opens the book to a sports section. "I'm told your Dad was a great basketball player."

"Yeah, sure, he told me all the time, especially his left jump shot." I laugh. "You know I never heard him boasting about himself to other people, but he sure did to me about basketball. Especially when we shot hoops in the driveway. Whenever he missed one, I'd razz him like, 'Hey, I thought you had a good jump shot, old man. You must be losing it.' Then he would throw the ball real hard at me and say something like, 'Show a little respect for the guy that put a ball in your hands before you could walk.'"

And suddenly, as often happens, I miss him so much. No one says anything.

Then Rosetta turns the page. The photo shows the Middleville cheerleaders in a pyramid in their white sweaters with big green M's. Four white girls and a black girl on top. "Is that you?" I ask.

I look closer. Of course it is. Her big smile.

She nods to me to indicate a yes.

Now Luther takes the book from his mother and looks at it also. "Mom, that pyramid looks pretty shaky. Did it hold up?"

Rosetta laughs in what sounds to me like a nervous giggle. "We had a few collapses as I recall."

Why are we looking at the yearbook now, and why did Mom lead me in here to do that? We're joking around one minute, but then everyone gets quiet. Luther clears his throat. Rosetta goes from a nervous giggle to what looks like tears in her eyes.

I look at Mom as if to ask, "What's going on?" So I say, "Is there something going on here that I don't know about?"

Mom says, "Since you put it that way, yes, there is. Not going on right now, but went on many years ago, and we want you to know about it. You deserve to know."

Rosetta lets out a deep breath. "Mary, I'll tell Teddy, if that's okay with you."

Mom says, "Please, that might be best."

Rosetta says, "Teddy, the reason we're here alone in this room is so we can tell you that your dad and I did know each other in high school. We had a chemistry class together…and well, we also had *chemistry*, you might say." Another big sigh. "We became close friends and would have dated but that wasn't allowed in the sixties."

I glance at each face in the room, and everyone looks like they're holding their breaths.

Rosetta goes on. "So we never dated but we did speak often. Almost every day. And we found a way to see each other secretly."

Then I remember what Luther told me. His dad was a white boy. A white boy from Middelburg in his mom's class. "Wait a minute. Are you saying what I think…?"

They all nod their heads at the same time.

"Oh my gosh, why didn't anyone tell me this?" I'm confused and I feel a little bit angry. "Everyone knew this but me?" I look directly at Mom.

Mom says, "Not everyone." She looks around. "Just those of us in this room. We wanted to tell you and Luther both at the same time. But it was the very night you came home from winning that basketball game where you thought Dad watched you from above, and you were so proud to be his son. His only son. I didn't have the heart to tell you that night, but Rosetta had already told Luther…and—" Her voice trails off and now the tears stream down her face. "And then it never seemed like the right time, and you were still grieving so much for your dad."

Whenever Mom cries, I want to hug her. So I go to her and sit beside her. I put my arm around her shoulders which feel so thin. My brief anger disappears. "It's okay, Mom. Really, it is. Please don't cry."

Rosetta says, "After 9/11, we knew we shouldn't wait any longer. How sad it would have been never to have known you had a brother

I step back and peer at Luther who also has his arm around his mother like he wants to protect her. And when I look at his face, for the first time, I see it. The resemblance. So obvious. The dimple in his chin—just like Dad's.

No one says anything. They are waiting for my reaction. Their eyes seek me out. Rosetta's dark brown eyes, Mom's blue eyes, Luther's hazel eyes—Dad's eyes. And I feel something stirring deep inside me that I didn't even know was there. It's filling my chest with a yearning I can't describe. I don't know exactly what joy feels like, but I think that's what this might be. I can't catch my breath, so I don't try to speak.

I simply walk over to Luther, and he stands up to meet me. I hug him as hard as I can. He's a little taller than me and my head hits his shoulder. I feel a sob escaping. He hugs me back so hard I start to laugh in relief, and then we are all laughing and crying at the same time. It's a beautiful sound.

Luther pushes me away from him slightly, puts both hands on my shoulders and looks me in the eye. He says, "Hello, little brother."

Epilogue
NEW YEAR'S EVE 2001

We are gathered at Baba's house for our traditional New Year's Eve celebration. I play a mix of songs on the new iPod I got for Christmas. On October 23, Apple came out with the slogan, *1000 songs in your pocket.* Of course, every teen wanted one, and I certainly dropped enough hints.

We've had two New Years' celebrations now without Dad, and this year we are also missing Rosetta's mother, Charlotte. But by this time next year, we'll have a new addition as Luther and Marletta are expecting a baby this summer. Everyone is suggesting names. Because of 9/11, Mindy says if it's a girl, she should be called Liberty—Libby for short.

"We have an announcement," says Luther, before our traditional champagne toast at midnight.

"It's twins?" Mindy pipes up eagerly. "Now you can name one Liberty and the other one Freedom. Freddy for short." Everyone laughs and Marletta rolls her eyes.

I come to Mindy's defense. "You'll have to excuse Mindy. She got into the bubbly before everyone else."

Mindy looks at me. "And what's wrong with my idea?"

I say, "It's goofy, like you." I put one arm around her and clasp the other hand over her mouth while I kiss the top of her curly red mop. "Baba, where do you keep your duct tape?"

Marletta and Luther look at each other. "You tell them, Marletta."

She says, "No, you say it."

Luther looks at Rosetta and Dr. Stone, who conveniently are standing together.

"We've decided on a name if our baby is a girl. She will be named after both our grandmothers, Charlotte May."

Rosetta claps her hands together and gives out a little squeal. "I love it," she says.

Dr. Stone passes her his handkerchief after he dabs his own eyes with it.

Marletta's mother, May, says, "That's a beautiful honor. Thank you, Marletta."

It's almost midnight and Mom and Mike start filling our fancy flutes with champagne. Fancy like the plastic throw-away kind from the new dollar store in town. The usual sparkling apple cider fills the flutes for Cathy and Ruby.

As always, Uncle Dan makes the toast, "A blessed New Year to all in this home…all in this family. We remember those who are no longer with us, Stan and Charlotte." He raises his glass to Dr. Stone.

He continues. "And we welcome Luther to our family this year."

Mom and Rosetta told Uncle Dan and Baba the whole story shortly after they told me. Once Baba got over the shock, she was thrilled at the thought of another grandson and welcomed Luther with open arms. Her first words were, "Luther, now I cook for you."

Dan goes on. "And we look forward to our newest arrival in 2002." He smiles and nods to Luther and Marletta.

"And on this New Year's 2001, we think of all the families who are missing loved ones tonight, those lost in the World Trade Center, and ask that God bless them and keep them safe. And bless our beautiful America and keep it safe."

The TV starts playing "Auld Lang Syne" as Baba's grandfather clock strikes midnight. We lift our glasses and hug and kiss one another with New Year's wishes, and then join in the singing.

Toward the end of the first verse, I find the remote and mute the TV. Then I grab a fork from one of the appetizer platters and clink it on my glass, forgetting that it is plastic. So I walk to the dining room table and clink it on the side of an appetizer platter. "While we're all together here, I'd like to make an announcement too." I take a deep breath.

"Teddy, are *you* pregnant" Mindy asks. Everyone laughs and I have to clink the plate again.

I clear my throat. "I know it's a tradition in this family that the men go to Indiana University."

"Go Boilermakers," shouts my cousin, Sophie, who recently transferred from IU to Purdue to study engineering.

"I said *men*, Sophie, so you are excused from that tradition." Now that I have their attention, I continue. "There's another tradition in our family that I want to honor and carry on. Baba, you and Papa escaped communism in your homeland, Bulgaria, and started over in a new country where you didn't have any family or even speak the language. You came for a better life, not only for yourselves but for the children you would have. And because you were so brave to do so, we are now here in this wonderful country.

"I want to be brave too. So..." I take one more deep breath. "I've decided that instead of starting college this fall, which would have been IU, of course—" I nod to Sophie, then hesitate...another deep breath. "As soon as I graduate, I am joining the Marines."

A silence falls.

I look at George who, although he looks like he is about to cry, gives me a thumbs-up sign. My voice breaks and I stifle a sob. "I want to defend my country so we can keep having the freedoms so many immigrants came here for. And so there is never another 9/11 on our soil—the soil, I'm told, my great grandfather kissed when he stepped onto Ellis Island."

There is a hush in the room and I glance at Mom first. She has raised her hands to her eyes. "Mom, I'm sorry if I am disappoint...."

"Disappoint? Teddy, I could not be more proud of you than I am at this moment."

Then everyone, as if they needed Mom's blessing, starts clapping. Uncle Dan wipes his eyes also, and Luther comes over and gives me a big hug while he whispers in my ear, "I am so proud to call you my brother."

THE END

Index

The stories George told Teddy are true stories from Don Armour's childhood memoir, *A Perfect Childhood*, that he wrote for his family. Here are some of his other favorite sayings:

Uglier than a mud fence in a hail storm
Dumber than a box of rocks
Bigger than a barrel
Couldn't hit the broad side of a barn even if you were inside it and the doors were closed
Older than dirt
You look sharper than a mashed tater sandwich
Smoother than a school marm's thigh
I'm falling apart like a K-Mart shirt
It's darker than the inside of a cow
I'm busier than a one-arm paper hanger
It's raining like a cow peeing on a flat rock
Off like a dirty shirt
Hungry enough to eat the south end of a skunk headed north
Off like a herd of turtles
We're burning daylight
Better than a poke in the eye with a sharp stick
Finer than frog's hair

The Twelve Days of Christmas Gifts

These were actually brought to Pages Book Store in Ahwatukee by the Davis family—Rita, Ken, Kenneth and Katie.

On the first day of Christmas, your true loves say to you—"Can't catch me 'cause I'm too fast." Gingerbread man cookie.

On the second day of Christmas, your true friends bring to you—"Two turtledoves and we hope you enjoyed your gingerbread man." A box of Turtles candy.

On the third day of Christmas, your true friends bring to you—"Three French hens." Three Cornish game hens.

Four calling birds picked these for you to enjoy on the fourth day of Christmas. A cluster of Bing cherries.

On the fifth day of Christmas, your true friends bring to you—five golden rings. Homemade donuts, warm and fresh.

On the sixth day of Christmas, your true friends bring to you—six geese a-laying. Two potholders with three geese on each of them.

On the seventh day of Christmas, your true friends bring to you—seven swans a-swimming. It's too cold to swim, but if you brave it, here's a towel to dry off with. A hand towel with Santa on it.

On the eighth day of Christmas, your true friends bring to you—eight cows a-milking. Chocolate milk mix. *Have you ever tried milking a chocolate cow?*

On the ninth day of Christmas, your true friends brought to you—nine candy canes. 'Cause we didn't know what else to do.

On the tenth day of Christmas, your true friends bring to you—ten little froggies. If you give them a magical kiss, they will turn into ten lords a-leaping—a little frog toy for the bathtub and some cookies.

On the eleventh day of Christmas, your true friends bring to you—ten drummers drumming. A drum to hang on your Christmas tree, and we hope you hear the beautiful music of Christmas—the little drum ornament and a cassette of Christmas carols.

On the twelfth day of Christmas, your true friends bring to you—one little teddy Bear who couldn't keep up with the leaping lords—one stuffed bear perched on top of the warm teddy-bear pumpkin cake.

Merry Christmas from the Ken Davis family.

Recipes

Baba's Baklava

1 pound <u>phyllo pastry</u>, thawed if frozen

1 cup <u>butter</u>, melted at room temp

$\frac{3}{4}$ cup <u>sugar</u>

1 teaspoon <u>ground cinnamon</u>

2 cups chopped <u>walnuts</u>

$\frac{1}{2}$ cup <u>water</u>

$\frac{1}{4}$ cup <u>lemon juice</u>

$\frac{1}{4}$ cup <u>honey</u>

Preheat oven to 325. Layer half of the sheets of phyllo, one sheet at a time, in a greased 11 x 7 x 2 baking pan, brushing each sheet evenly with butter and folding ends over if necessary to fit into pan.

Keep unused sheets covered with plastic wrap while assembling baklava to prevent drying.

Mix 1/4 cup of the sugar and cinnamon; stir in walnuts.

Sprinkle nut mixture evenly over buttered phyllo in pan.

Layer remaining phyllo, one sheet at a time, over nut mixture, brushing each sheet evenly with butter.

Cut diagonally into squares, cutting completely through all layers.

Bake in preheated oven until crisp and golden, about one hour.

Combine remaining sugar, water, lemon juice and honey in small saucepan; cook and stir over low heat until sugar dissolves.

Heat to boiling; pour evenly over hot baklava.

Let stand loosely covered eight hours or overnight.

***

Davis Family Gooey Pumpkin Cake

1 box Betty Crocker™ Super Moist™ yellow cake mix

8 tablespoons (1 stick) unsalted butter, melted and cooled slightly

1 egg

Filling:

1 package (8 oz) package cream cheese, softened

1 can (15 oz) pumpkin

8 tablespoons (1 stick) unsalted butter, melted and cooled slightly

1 teaspoon vanilla

3 eggs

1 box or bag (16 oz) powdered sugar

2 teaspoons pumpkin pie spice

Caramel sauce and candied pecans, for topping

Gather your ingredients and heat oven to 350°F. Line 9 x 13 pan with parchment paper, then lightly spray pan with cooking spray.

Cake base: In a large bowl or bowl of a stand mixer, beat cake mix, melted butter and egg until well combined. Spread and press batter evenly into bottom of prepared pan.

Filling: In another large bowl (or clean bowl of a stand mixer), beat cream cheese and pumpkin until well combined. Add melted butter, vanilla and eggs; stir until combined. Stir in powdered sugar and pumpkin pie spice until combined. Pour batter evenly into pan over cake base.

Bake 1 hour to 1 hour 15 minutes, until center of cake is just set and slightly wobbly (if using a 13 x 9-inch pan, lessen the baking time). Cool completely on a cooling rack.

Serve slices of cake with caramel sauce and candied pecans on top.

James' Braised Short Ribs

5 pounds bone-in beef short ribs, cut crosswise into 2-inch pieces

Kosher salt and freshly ground black pepper

3 tablespoons vegetable oil

3 medium onions, chopped

3 medium carrots, peeled, chopped

2 celery stalks, chopped

3 tablespoons all-purpose flour

1 tablespoon tomato paste

1 750-ml bottle dry red wine (preferably cabernet sauvignon)

10 sprigs flat-leaf parsley

8 sprigs thyme

4 sprigs oregano

2 sprigs rosemary

2 fresh or dried bay leaves

1 head of garlic, halved crosswise

4 cups low-salt beef stock

Preheat oven to 350°.

Season short ribs with salt and pepper. Heat oil in a large Dutch oven over medium-high. Working in two batches, brown short ribs on all sides, about eight minutes per batch. Transfer short ribs to a plate. Pour off all but three tablespoons' drippings from pot.

Add onions, carrots, and celery to pot and cook over medium-high heat, stirring often, until onions are browned, about five minutes.

Add flour and tomato paste; cook, stirring constantly, until well combined and deep red, two to three minutes.

Stir in wine, then add short ribs with any accumulated juices. Bring to a boil; lower heat to medium and simmer until wine is reduced by half, about twenty-five minutes.

Add all herbs to pot along with garlic. Stir in stock. Bring to a boil, cover, and transfer to oven.

Cook until short ribs are tender, 2–2½ hours. Transfer short ribs to a platter. Strain sauce from pot into a measuring cup. Spoon fat from surface of sauce and discard; season sauce to taste with salt and pepper.

Serve in shallow bowls over mashed potatoes with sauce spooned over.

Rosetta's Gorgonzola/Apple/Lettuce Salad

1 head romaine or Bibb lettuce or combination-chopped

Walnuts chopped in half. Can be toasted with touch of butter and sugar or plain

Gorgonzola cheese crumbles

Green apple cut in bite size pieces

Grape tomatoes cut in half

Crisp crumbled bacon (optional)

Poppy seed dressing

Place chopped lettuce in bowl or on small platter

Add other ingredients and top with poppy seed dressing. This is best assembled for each salad individually so toppings don't fall to bottom of the large salad mixing bowl.

James' Crostini Appetizer

1 container grape tomatoes cut in half

2 oz cream cheese

6 oz feta cheese crumbled

2/3 cup olive oil (divided)

2 tablespoons minced shallot

Chopped basil

Slices of baguette bread cut on diagonal about ¼ inch thick

2 tablespoons pine nuts

Brown pine nuts them briefly on stovetop. Watch them as they burn easily.

Combine tomatoes with shallots, garlic, vinegar and let sit for about five minutes.

Stir in basil and 1/3 cup olive oil, salt and pepper. Let sit ten minutes

Brush bread with remaining olive oil and put under broiler for a just a minute

Spread cheese mixture on breads. Top with grape tomato mixture. Sprinkle pine nuts on top.

Baba's Tacos

4 pounds of beef and pork mixed and cubed into small chunks

2 chopped onions

2 cloves garlic chopped

1 tsp ground cumin seed

1½ tablespoons flour

½-can crushed tomatoes (the big 303-can size)

1/3 cup water

Brown meat. Add onions and garlic.

Add flour to meat and stir.

Mash tomatoes into mixture and add water.

Add cumin seed

Cook until tender (between one to one-and-a-half hours)

Sauce:

1/2 can tomatoes (other half of the 303)

1/3 can water

1 chopped onion

2 cloves garlic chopped

1 tablespoon chili powder

1 tablespoon red ground pepper or flakes

1 package chili or taco mix

Brown onions in a little oil.

Add all other ingredients and mix meat and sauce together after meat is cooked. Stir well and heat together.

Baba's Tamale Corn

2 cans cream-style corn

2 eggs

¾ cup cornmeal

2 small cans green chilis

½ teaspoon baking powder

¾ teaspoon garlic salt

6 tablespoons salad oil

6 oz grated cheddar cheese

Mix all ingredients together in a baking casserole sprayed with non-stick spray.

Bake at 375 degrees for one hour.

For more of Baba's recipes see Index in first book, *I'll Always Be With You* or visit Violetta's

blog: www.serendipity-reflections.